Blackstone Outdoor Gas Griddle Cookbook for Beginners

The Ultimate Guide to Master You Blackstone Outdoor Gas Griddle with 150 Tasty Recipes

Baran Sedorik

Table of Contents

Introduction

The Blackstone griddle is founded and started to manufactured different types of the griddle in 2005. They manufactured flagship griddle and the product made by Blackstone are bestseller products available in the market. The quality of products is the design and manufactured in the USA. In this book, we have used Blackstone outdoor gas griddle to cook delicious griddle dishes.

The Blackstone gas griddle is built-up from quality stainless steel material and lasts a lifetime. The upper cooking surface is made from a steel griddle top. The overall built quality of the griddle is the flagship level. The 36-inch model loaded with 4 large size burners given with a separate controller switch for each burner. The Blackstone gas griddle uses a propane gas tank as a griddle fuel. Due to the large cooking surface area, the griddle is capable to cook a large amount of food at a time. Different temperature controller allows you to cook foods at different temperature settings at the same time. The Blackstone gas griddle is an ideal choice for cooking food at weekend parties. The book contains all the information about the Blackstone gas griddle. How to season your gas griddle? What kind of tools used while using the gas griddle? What are the benefits of Blackstone gas griddle and how to clean, store, and maintain your gas griddle for a long time?

The book contains 100 delicious and tasty recipes from different categories like breakfast, poultry, beef pork and lamb, fish and seafood, vegetables and side dishes, snacks, and game recipes. All the recipes are unique and written in an easily understandable form. The recipes are written with their number of servings, preparation, and cooking time information. Each recipe ends with its exact nutritional value information. The nutritional value information will help you to keep track of daily calorie consumption. There are various cookbooks available on this topic thanks for choosing my cookbook I hope you love and enjoy all the recipes written in this cookbook.

Chapter 1: Blackstone Outdoor Gas Griddle Basics

Blackstone Outdoor Gas Griddle

Blackstone is a leading manufacturer of outdoor griddle which improves your outdoor cooking experience. They are one of the top industry leader's manufactures in the USA made outdoor gas griddles since 2005. The Blackstone outdoor griddle or grills are one of the best-selling flagship products available in the USA market.

The Blackstone outdoor gas griddle is one of the best affordable gas griddle devices compare to other devices available in the market. It is available in two different sizes one is 28 inch and the other is 36-inch size. The 28-inch gas griddle made up of stainless steel frame comes with a 470 square inch cooking surface area. The gas griddle is loaded with two H-shape large size gas burners each burner can produce 15000 BTU and both the burner's together produce 30000 BTU heat. The 36-inch gas griddle offers a 720 square inch large size cooking area to cook a whole family food at a time. The gas griddle is loaded with four H-shape large size gas burners. All together these burners can produce 6000 BTU of heat. All the burners are equipped with separate controller switch so you can easily controller them independently.

The Blackstone gas griddle is easy to assemble and built up with high-quality stainless steel coated with black powder coating. The main cooking surface area is made up of thick rolled steel material. The griddle has a battery power ignition system started by just push-button ignition and capable to produce a maximum 350 °F temperature. The four heavy-duty burners heat-up the cooking area very fast. The Blackstone gas griddle comes with a bottom shelf and two convenient side-mounted shelves and a propane tank holder. You can easily move the gas griddle outdoor cooking appliance with the help of four caster wheels. You can lock two wheels among these four wheels to keep your appliance steady in your backyard.

Its large 720 square inches cooking surface area is capable to handle a large quantity of food. It is capable to hold 16 steaks, 72 hot dogs, and 28 hamburgers at a time. It is also capable to cook two different foods at the same time but on different temperature settings.

When you cook eggs it is not suitable to cook it at 60000BTU heat but at the same temperature settings is suitable for steak. The griddle allows you to individually control all four heating zones as per your recipe needs at the same time.

Seasoning Your Blackstone Griddle

When you buy a new griddle, it is recommended that before using the griddle season it with proper seasoning method to make a non-stick layer over the cooking area and avoid scratching while cooking your food. You just need to follow the simple seasoning steps given below to improve your griddle cooking efficiency. Before starting seasoning make sure you have collected all items and supplies needed during the seasoning process. These items and supplies include a Bucket of water, tongs or heatproof gloves, soap powder, salt, stick, and cast iron conditioner.

1. Clean your brand new griddle with soapy water

Take 2 liters of warm water into a bucket and some soap. Mix the soap and water solution with the help of a stick. Then pour a small amount of soapy water over the griddle cooking surface and thoroughly rub it over the griddle surface with the help of a paper towel.

If you are using an old griddle then skip this soapy water step this step may damage the coating area of the griddle.

2. Heat the griddle for 10 t0 15 minutes

Turn on all the burners with its maximum temperature settings and allow the griddle heat up for 10 to 15 minutes. After some time you will notice that the top of the griddle turns brown. Then move to the next step.

3. Spread oil over griddle surface

You can choose your favorite oil for seasoning griddle. Always use high fatty acid oil like extra virgin olive oil, vegetable oil, coconut oil, flaxseed oil, and more to coat your griddle. Take 2 to 3 tablespoon of oil and spread them over the griddle surface. Use a paper towel to spread the oil equally all over the griddle surface. You can also use a highly recommended cast iron conditioner for the coating griddle surface. Then move to the next step.

4. Fire the griddle again

Ignite all the burners at its max temperature position and allow it for 15 to 30 minutes at max setting. You will notice the griddle turns black after some time and the oil begin smoking when it reaches its smoke point. Wait until the smoke will completely disappear.

5. Turn of griddle

Turn off the griddle after completing the first cycle and let it cool down at least 10 minutes. After that repeat the same procedure again and again until the griddle is turned dark brown. It requires 3 to 4 repetitions.

6. Final touch

Wipe the griddle with high quality extra virgin oil or cast iron conditioner to prevent it from oxidation. Now your griddle seasoning process is completed successfully.

Essential Tools for Griddle

Three main necessary tools make you master in griddle cooking. These tools are oil bottles, Spatula, and Scrapers which makes outdoor griddle cooking easy. You can also use extra tools if you want to baste, steam, press, and blacken your food.

1. Spatula

It is one of the necessary tools used to flip, spread, mix, and lift your favorite foods like pancakes, burgers, eggs, veggies, omelets, and more. It is one kind of flat, broad, and flexible tool with an ergonomic handle made up of sturdy stainless steel material and available in large, medium, and small sizes.

2. Scraper

Scraper is a sharp blade-like tool used to clean your griddle surface for derbies. The scraper is a wide stainless steel blade comes with an ergonomic sleep resistant grip which provides perfect control when scrapping and digging over a griddle.

3. Squeeze Bottles

Squeeze bottles are easy tools to spread oils, sausage, and water while griddles your food. The squeeze bottles are made up of high-quality BPA-free plastic.

4. Round Basting Cover

The blasting cover is made up of stainless steel material and comes with a safety handle. A blasting cover is a multipurpose tool used to steam veggies, melting cheese, and more. Use a 12-inch big-size blasting cover that is capable to hold a large portion of your food and number of patties at a time.

5. Bacon Grill Press

The grill press is made up of cast iron and comes with a wooden handle grip for safety purposes. It is idle for making flatten bacon, hamburgers, sandwiches, and also used as a steak weight. The main purpose of using a press grill is to remove out excess grease from burgers.

Benefits of Using Blackstone Outdoor Gas Griddle

There are lots of benefits to cooking your food on a Blackstone outdoor gas griddle. Let's see all these benefits one by one.

1. Large and Flat Surface Cooking

One of the main benefits of the Blackstone gas griddle is its large and flat cooking surface. The large cooking area allows you to cook more food items to cook at once and flip food is easy to compare to a frying pan. You can use the griddle to cook a large quantity of food. The Blackstone griddle is capable to hold 72 hotdogs, 28 hamburgers, and 16 steaks in a single cooking batch. Due to the large cooking surface, it doesn't hold moisture and gives you a crispy cooking result. It is one of the perfect choices for bigger families who love to enjoy food like eggs, bacon, hotdogs, burgers, and veggies at the same time in backyard parties.

2. Excellent built quality

The Blackstone gas grills are made up of high-quality stainless steel materials. The main cooking surface is made up of rolled high quality 7 gauge steel. The entire body surface is covered with a black powder coating which protects it from rust.

3. Runs on Propane gas

The Blackstone gas grills use propane gas to cook your food. Compare to charcoal fuel propane gas never creates smoke and harmful gases while cooking food in your backyard. Propane griddles are easy to start all you just need to turn the dial and the burner fired up. The gas griddle is capable to maintain a steady temperature. Your griddle takes less than 15 minutes to reaches its maximum temperature.

4. Versatile

The Blackstone gas griddle is one of the versatile outdoor cooking appliances offers to cook most of the foods over a smooth cooking surface. The Blackstone gas griddle is equipped with 4 burners which allow you to operate them individually. The griddle is capable to cook different types of food at a different temperature at the same time. You can make pancakes, eggs, waffles, steak, burgers, hot dogs, and more with perfection on Blackstone gas griddle.

5. Easy to clean

To clean the Blackstone griddle is one of the easy tasks you just need to clean the greasy cooking area. To clean grease you can use a spatula or griddle to scrap up grease. Use a paper towel to wipe the cooking surface and finally give the touch-up with a scouring pad.

How to Store and Maintain Your Seasoned Griddle Properly?

The proper storage and maintenance are necessary to increase the lifespan of your griddle. The following steps guide you for the storage and maintenance of your griddle.

1. After each use clean your griddle

When you start using your griddle it seasons automatically after each use. Cleaning is one of the important steps to keep your griddle clean and hygiene. Use hot water and a paper towel to clean the griddle surface. Do not use soapy water to clean the cooking surface use scrapper to clean the cooking area. You can clean the greasy surface with clean and dry paper towels.

2. Remove Rust

If you find any rust spot over the griddle then use 40 or 60 low grit sandpaper or you can also use steel wool to remove the rust spot scrub them properly.

3. Coat griddle after cleaning

After finishing the cleaning process give a thin coat of cooking spray over the griddle cooking surface to prevent rusting built up the overcooking surface area of the griddle.

4. Store and Maintain griddle

After finishing all the cleaning steps store your griddle in a cool and dry place. To prevent dust always keep your griddle into cover and keep it away from the humid area.

Chapter 2: Breakfast

Almond Pancakes

Preparation Time: 10 minutes
Cooking Time: 10 minutes
Serve: 2

Ingredients:

- 1 egg
- 1/2 cup almond flour
- 1/2 tsp baking powder
- 1/2 tbsp heavy whipping cream
- 1 1/2 tbsp Swerve

Directions:

1. Preheat the griddle to medium-low heat.
2. In a bowl, mix almond flour, Baking powder, sweetener, and salt.
3. In another bowl, whisk egg and heavy whipping cream.
4. Add dry ingredients into the wet and mix well.
5. Spray griddle top with cooking spray.
6. Drop batter onto the hot griddle top.
7. Cook pancakes until lightly golden brown from both sides.
8. Serve and enjoy.

Nutritional Value (Amount per Serving):

- Calories 90
- Fat 7 g
- Carbohydrates 13 g
- Sugar 11 g
- Protein 4 g
- Cholesterol 87 mg

French Toast Sticks

Preparation Time: 10 minutes

Cooking Time: 10 minutes

Serve: 2

Ingredients:

- 2 eggs
- 4 bread slices, cut each bread slice into 3 pieces vertically
- 2/3 cup milk
- 1/4 tsp ground cinnamon
- 1 tsp vanilla

Directions:

1. Preheat the griddle to medium-low heat.
2. In a bowl, whisk eggs with cinnamon, vanilla, and milk.
3. Spray griddle top with cooking spray.
4. Dip each bread piece into the egg mixture and coat well.
5. Place coated bread pieces onto the hot griddle top and cook until golden brown from both sides.
6. Serve and enjoy.

Nutritional Value (Amount per Serving):

- Calories 166
- Fat 7 g
- Carbohydrates 14 g
- Sugar 5 g
- Protein 10.4 g
- Cholesterol 193 mg

Simple Cheese Sandwich

Preparation Time: 10 minutes

Cooking Time: 10 minutes

Serve: 1

Ingredients:

- 2 bread slices
- 2 tsp butter
- 2 cheese slices

Directions:

1. Preheat the griddle to medium-low heat.
2. Place cheese slices on top of one bread slice and cover cheese with another bread slice.
3. Spread butter on top of both the bread slices.
4. Place sandwich on hot griddle top and cook until golden brown or until cheese is melted.
5. Serve and enjoy.

Nutritional Value (Amount per Serving):

- Calories 340
- Fat 26 g
- Carbohydrates 9.8 g
- Sugar 1 g
- Protein 15.4 g
- Cholesterol 79 mg

Cauliflower Fritters

Preparation Time: 10 minutes
Cooking Time: 15 minutes
Serve: 6

Ingredients:

- 2 eggs
- 1 large head cauliflower, cut into florets
- 1 tbsp butter
- 1/2 tsp turmeric
- 1 tbsp nutritional yeast
- 2/3 cup almond flour
- 1/4 tsp black pepper
- 1/2 tsp salt

Directions:

1. Add cauliflower florets to a large pot.
2. Pour enough water to cover the cauliflower florets. Bring to boil for 8-10 minutes.
3. Drain cauliflower well and transfer in food processor and process until it looks like rice.
4. Transfer cauliflower rice into the large bowl.
5. Add remaining ingredients except for butter to the bowl and stir to combine.
6. Preheat the griddle to medium heat.
7. Melt butter onto the hot griddle top.
8. Make small patties from cauliflower mixture and place on hot griddle top and cook for 3-4 minutes on each side or until lightly golden brown.
9. Serve and enjoy.

Nutritional Value (Amount per Serving):

- Calories 155
- Fat 10 g
- Carbohydrates 11.1 g
- Sugar 3.9 g
- Protein 8.1 g
- Cholesterol 60 mg

Easy Banana Pancakes

Preparation Time: 10 minutes

Cooking Time: 10 minutes

Serve: 6

Ingredients:

- 2 eggs
- 2 tbsp vanilla protein powder
- 1 large banana, mashed
- 1/8 tsp baking powder

Directions:

1. Preheat the griddle to medium-low heat.
2. Meanwhile, add all ingredients into the bowl and mix well until combined.
3. Spray griddle top with cooking spray.
4. Pour 3 tablespoons of batter onto hot griddle top to make a pancake.
5. Cook pancake until lightly browned from both sides.
6. Serve and enjoy.

Nutritional Value (Amount per Serving):

- Calories 79
- Fat 1.6 g
- Carbohydrates 5.5 g
- Sugar 3 g
- Protein 11 g
- Cholesterol 55 mg

Cauliflower Hash Browns

Preparation Time: 10 minutes
Cooking Time: 10 minutes
Serve: 6

Ingredients:

- 1 egg
- 3 cups cauliflower, grated
- 3/4 cup cheddar cheese, shredded
- 1/8 tsp pepper
- 1/4 tsp garlic powder
- 1/4 tsp cayenne pepper
- 1/2 tsp salt

Directions:

1. Preheat the griddle to medium-low heat.
2. Add all ingredients into the bowl and mix well.
3. Spray griddle top with cooking spray.
4. Make 6 hash browns from mixture and place on hot griddle top and cook until golden brown from both sides.
5. Serve and enjoy.

Nutritional Value (Amount per Serving):

- Calories 80
- Fat 5 g
- Carbohydrates 3 g
- Sugar 1 g
- Protein 5 g
- Cholesterol 46 mg

Tomato Scrambled Egg

Preparation Time: 10 minutes

Cooking Time: 5 minutes

Serve: 2

Ingredients:

- 2 eggs, lightly beaten
- 2 tbsp fresh basil, chopped
- 1 tbsp olive oil
- 1/2 tomato, chopped
- Pepper
- Salt

Directions:

1. Preheat the griddle to medium heat.
2. Add oil on top of the griddle.
3. Add tomatoes and cook until softened.
4. Whisk eggs with basil, pepper, and salt.
5. Pour egg mixture on top of tomatoes and cook until eggs are set.
6. Serve and enjoy.

Nutritional Value (Amount per Serving):

- Calories 125
- Fat 12 g
- Carbohydrates 1 g
- Sugar 0.8 g
- Protein 5.8 g
- Cholesterol 164 mg

Caprese Omelet

Preparation Time: 10 minutes
Cooking Time: 10 minutes
Serve: 2

Ingredients:

- 6 eggs
- 3 oz cherry tomatoes, cut in halves
- 1 tbsp fresh basil
- 5 oz mozzarella cheese, sliced
- Pepper
- Salt

Directions:

1. Preheat the griddle to medium-low heat
2. Whisk eggs in a bowl with pepper and salt. Stir in basil.
3. Spray griddle top with cooking spray.
4. Add tomatoes on hot griddle top and sauté for few minutes.
5. Pour egg mixture on top of tomatoes and wait until eggs are slightly firm.
6. Add mozzarella cheese slices on top and let the omelet set.
7. Serve and enjoy.

Nutritional Value (Amount per Serving):

- Calories 515
- Fat 40 g
- Carbohydrates 5.2 g
- Sugar 2.1 g
- Protein 37 g
- Cholesterol 529 mg

Pumpkin Pancake

Preparation Time: 10 minutes

Cooking Time: 10 minutes

Serve: 4

Ingredients:

- 4 eggs
- 1/2 tsp cinnamon
- 1/2 cup pumpkin puree
- 1 cup almond flour
- 2 tsp liquid stevia
- 1 tsp baking powder

Directions:

1. Preheat the griddle to medium-low heat.
2. In a bowl, mix almond flour, stevia, baking powder, cinnamon, pumpkin puree, and eggs until well combined.
3. Spray griddle top with cooking spray.
4. Drop batter onto the hot griddle top.
5. Cook pancakes until lightly golden brown from both sides.
6. Serve and enjoy.

Nutritional Value (Amount per Serving):

- Calories 235
- Fat 18.5 g
- Carbohydrates 9.6 g
- Sugar 2.4 g
- Protein 11.9 g
- Cholesterol 164 mg

Easy Cheese Omelet

Preparation Time: 10 minutes

Cooking Time: 10 minutes

Serve: 2

Ingredients:

- 6 eggs
- 7 oz cheddar cheese, shredded
- 3 oz butter
- Pepper
- Salt

Directions:

1. In a bowl, whisk together eggs, half cheese, pepper, and salt.
2. Preheat the griddle to medium heat.
3. Melt butter on the hot griddle top.
4. Once butter is melted then pour egg mixture onto the griddle top and cook until set.
5. Add remaining cheese fold and serve.

Nutritional Value (Amount per Serving):

- Calories 892
- Fat 80 g
- Carbohydrates 2.4 g
- Sugar 1.6 g
- Protein 41.7 g
- Cholesterol 687 mg

Spinach Pancakes

Preparation Time: 10 minutes

Cooking Time: 10 minutes

Serve: 6

Ingredients:

- 4 eggs
- 1 cup coconut milk
- 1/4 cup chia seeds
- 1 cup spinach, chopped
- 1/2 tsp black pepper
- 1/2 tsp ground nutmeg
- 1 tsp baking soda
- 1/2 cup coconut flour
- 1/2 tsp salt

Directions:

1. In a bowl, whisk eggs with coconut milk until frothy.
2. Mix together all dry ingredients and add in the egg mixture and whisk until smooth.
3. Add spinach and stir well.
4. Preheat the griddle to medium-low heat.
5. Spray griddle top with cooking spray.
6. Pour 3-4 tablespoons of batter onto the hot griddle top and make a round pancake.
7. Cook pancake until lightly golden brown from both sides.
8. Serve and enjoy.

Nutritional Value (Amount per Serving):

- Calories 111
- Fat 7 g
- Carbohydrates 5 g
- Sugar 0.4 g
- Protein 6.3 g
- Cholesterol 109 mg

Spicy Egg Scrambled

Preparation Time: 10 minutes
Cooking Time: 10 minutes
Serve: 2

Ingredients:

- 4 eggs
- 2 tbsp cilantro, chopped
- 1/3 cup heavy cream
- 1 tomato, diced
- 3 tbsp butter
- 1 Serrano chili pepper, chopped
- 2 tbsp scallions, sliced
- 1/4 tsp pepper
- 1/2 tsp salt

Directions:

1. Preheat the griddle to medium heat.
2. Melt butter on top of the hot griddle.
3. Add tomato and chili pepper and sauté for 2 minutes.
4. In a bowl, whisk eggs with cilantro, cream, pepper, and salt.
5. Pour egg mixture over tomato and chili pepper and stir until egg is set.
6. Garnish with scallions and serve.

Nutritional Value (Amount per Serving):

- Calories 355
- Fat 33 g
- Carbohydrates 3 g
- Sugar 1.7 g
- Protein 12 g
- Cholesterol 401 mg

Chocolate Pancake

Preparation Time: 10 minutes

Cooking Time: 10 minutes

Serve: 4

Ingredients:

- 2 eggs
- 1/2 tsp baking powder
- 2 tbsp erythritol
- 1 1/2 tbsp cocoa powder
- 1/4 cup ground flaxseed
- 2 tbsp water
- 1 tsp nutmeg
- 1 tsp cinnamon
- 1/4 tsp salt

Directions:

1. In a bowl, mix ground flaxseed, baking powder, erythritol, cocoa powder, spices, and salt.
2. Add eggs and stir well.
3. Add water and stir until batter is well combined.
4. Preheat the griddle to medium-low heat.
5. Spray griddle top with cooking spray.
6. Pour a large spoonful of batter on a hot griddle top and make a pancake.
7. Cook pancake for 3-4 minutes on each side.
8. Serve and enjoy.

Nutritional Value (Amount per Serving):

- Calories 138
- Fat 12 g
- Carbohydrates 11 g
- Sugar 8 g
- Protein 4.5 g
- Cholesterol 82 mg

Broccoli Omelet

Preparation Time: 10 minutes

Cooking Time: 10 minutes

Serve: 2

Ingredients:

- 4 eggs
- 1 cup broccoli, chopped and cooked
- 1 tbsp olive oil
- 1/4 tsp pepper
- 1/2 tsp salt

Directions:

1. In a bowl, beat eggs with pepper, and salt.
2. Preheat the griddle to medium heat. Add oil to the griddle top.
3. Pour broccoli and egg mixture onto the hot griddle top and cook until set. Flip omelet and cook until lightly golden brown.
4. Serve and enjoy.

Nutritional Value (Amount per Serving):

- Calories 203
- Fat 16 g
- Carbohydrates 4 g
- Sugar 1.5 g
- Protein 12 g
- Cholesterol 327 mg

Healthy Oatmeal Pancake

Preparation Time: 10 minutes

Cooking Time: 10 minutes

Serve: 2

Ingredients:

- 6 egg whites
- 1 cup steel-cut oats
- 1/4 tsp vanilla
- 1 cup Greek yogurt
- 1/2 tsp baking powder
- 1 tsp liquid stevia
- 1/4 tsp cinnamon

Directions:

1. Preheat the griddle to medium-low heat.
2. Add oats to a blender and blend until a fine powder is a form.
3. Add remaining ingredients into the blender and blend until well combined.
4. Spray griddle top with cooking spray.
5. Pour 1/4 cup batter onto the hot griddle top.
6. Cook pancake until golden brown from both sides.
7. Serve and enjoy.

Nutritional Value (Amount per Serving):

- Calories 295
- Fat 4 g
- Carbohydrates 37 g
- Sugar 9 g
- Protein 23 g
- Cholesterol 7 mg

Chapter 3: Poultry

Curried Chicken Kebabs

Preparation Time: 10 minutes
Cooking Time: 10 minutes
Serve: 4

Ingredients:

- 1 1/2 lbs chicken breasts, boneless & cut into 1-inch pieces
- 1/2 cup soy sauce
- 1 tbsp olive oil
- 1 tbsp curry powder
- 1 tbsp brown sugar
- 2 tbsp peanut butter

Directions:

1. Add chicken in a large zip-lock bag.
2. In a small, bowl mix soy sauce, olive oil, curry powder, brown sugar, and peanut butter and pour over chicken.
3. Seal bag and shake until chicken is well coated and place in the refrigerator for overnight.
4. Thread marinated chicken onto skewers.
5. Preheat the griddle to high heat.
6. Spray griddle top with cooking spray.
7. Place chicken skewers onto the hot griddle top and cook for 12-15 minutes. Turn frequently.
8. Serve and enjoy.

Nutritional Value (Amount per Serving):

- Calories 430
- Fat 20 g
- Carbohydrates 7 g
- Sugar 3.5 g
- Protein 53 g
- Cholesterol 151 mg

Tasty Chicken Patties

Preparation Time: 10 minutes
Cooking Time: 10 minutes
Serve: 4

Ingredients:

- 1 lb ground chicken
- 1/4 tsp red pepper flakes
- 1/2 tsp chili seasoning
- 1/2 tsp ground cumin
- 1 tsp paprika

Directions:

1. Add all ingredients into the large bowl and mix well to combine.
2. Make four small round patties from the mixture.
3. Preheat the griddle to high heat.
4. Spray griddle top with cooking spray.
5. Place patties on hot griddle top and cook for 5 minutes on each side.
6. Serve and enjoy.

Nutritional Value (Amount per Serving):

- Calories 219
- Fat 8 g
- Carbohydrates 0.8 g
- Sugar 0.1 g
- Protein 33 g
- Cholesterol 101 mg

Pesto Chicken Breasts

Preparation Time: 10 minutes
Cooking Time: 10 minutes
Serve: 6

Ingredients:

- 1 3/4 lbs chicken breasts, skinless, boneless, and slice
- 1/2 cup mozzarella cheese, shredded
- 1/4 cup basil pesto

Directions:

1. Add chicken and pesto in a bowl and mix well, cover and place in the refrigerator for 2-3 hours.
2. Preheat the griddle to high heat.
3. Spray griddle top with cooking spray.
4. Place marinated chicken on hot griddle top and cook until chicken is completely done.
5. Sprinkle cheese over chicken and serve.

Nutritional Value (Amount per Serving):

- Calories 305
- Fat 14 g
- Carbohydrates 0.8 g
- Sugar 0.7 g
- Protein 40 g
- Cholesterol 122 mg

Simple Chicken Fajita

Preparation Time: 10 minutes
Cooking Time: 15 minutes
Serve: 4

Ingredients:

- 1 lb chicken breast, boneless, skinless & sliced
- 2 tsp olive oil
- 1 onion, sliced
- 2 bell peppers, sliced
- 1/8 tsp cayenne
- 1 tsp cumin
- 2 tsp chili powder
- Pepper
- Salt

Directions:

1. Add chicken, onion, and sliced bell peppers into the bowl.
2. Add cayenne, cumin, chili powder, oil, pepper, and salt and toss well.
3. Preheat the griddle to medium heat.
4. Add chicken mixture onto the hot griddle top and cook until vegetables are tender and chicken is cooked.
5. Serve and enjoy.

Nutritional Value (Amount per Serving):

- Calories 185
- Fat 5 g
- Carbohydrates 8.1 g
- Sugar 4.3 g
- Protein 25.2 g
- Cholesterol 73 mg

Tasty Turkey Patties

Preparation Time: 10 minutes
Cooking Time: 15 minutes
Serve: 2

Ingredients:

- 8 oz ground turkey breast
- 2 tsp fresh oregano, chopped
- 2 garlic cloves, minced
- 1/2 tsp red pepper, crushed
- 1/4 tsp salt

Directions:

1. Preheat the griddle to medium heat.
2. Add ground turkey and remaining ingredients into the bowl and mix until well combined.
3. Spray griddle top with cooking spray.
4. Make 2 patties from the mixture and place onto the hot griddle top and cook until golden brown from both sides.
5. Serve and enjoy.

Nutritional Value (Amount per Serving):

- Calories 325
- Fat 19 g
- Carbohydrates 4 g
- Sugar 1.6 g
- Protein 33 g
- Cholesterol 84 mg

Chicken Veggie Stir Fry

Preparation Time: 10 minutes
Cooking Time: 10 minutes
Serve: 2

Ingredients:

- 6 oz chicken breast, boneless and cut into cubes
- 1/4 onion, sliced
- 1/2 bell pepper, chopped
- 1/2 zucchini, chopped
- 1 tbsp olive oil
- 1/4 tsp dried thyme
- 1/2 tsp garlic powder
- 1 tsp dried oregano

Directions:

1. Add all ingredients into the large bowl and toss well.
2. Preheat the griddle to medium heat.
3. Transfer chicken mixture onto the hot griddle top and cook until vegetables are tender and chicken is cooked.
4. Serve and enjoy.

Nutritional Value (Amount per Serving):

- Calories 186
- Fat 8 g
- Carbohydrates 5 g
- Sugar 4 g
- Protein 20 g
- Cholesterol 0 mg

Chicken & Broccoli Stir Fry

Preparation Time: 10 minutes

Cooking Time: 15 minutes

Serve: 4

Ingredients:

- 1 lb chicken breast, skinless, boneless, and cut into chunks
- 1 tbsp soy sauce
- 1 tbsp ginger, minced
- 1/2 tsp garlic powder
- 1 tbsp olive oil
- 1/2 onion, sliced
- 2 cups broccoli florets
- 2 tsp hot sauce
- 2 tsp vinegar
- 1 tsp sesame oil
- Pepper
- Salt

Directions:

1. Add all ingredients into the large mixing bowl and toss well.
2. Preheat the griddle to medium heat.
3. Spray griddle top with cooking spray.
4. Transfer chicken and broccoli mixture onto the hot griddle top and cook until broccoli is tender and chicken is cooked.
5. Serve and enjoy.

Nutritional Value (Amount per Serving):

- Calories 200
- Fat 7 g
- Carbohydrates 6 g
- Sugar 1.6 g
- Protein 26 g
- Cholesterol 73 mg

Greek Chicken

Preparation Time: 10 minutes
Cooking Time: 15 minutes
Serve: 2

Ingredients:

- 2 chicken breasts, skinless and boneless
- 2 tbsp olive oil
- 1 tsp Italian seasoning
- 1 1/2 cup grape tomatoes, cut in half
- 1/2 cup olives
- 1/4 tsp pepper
- 1/4 tsp salt

Directions:

1. Season chicken with Italian seasoning, pepper, and salt.
2. Preheat the griddle to medium-low heat. Add oil to the griddle top.
3. Add season chicken onto the hot griddle top and cook for 4-6 minutes on each side. Transfer chicken on a plate.
4. Add tomatoes and olives onto the griddle top cook for 2-4 minutes.
5. Pour olive and tomato mixture on top of the chicken and serve.

Nutritional Value (Amount per Serving):

- Calories 468
- Fat 29.4 g
- Carbohydrates 7.8 g
- Sugar 3.8 g
- Protein 43.8 g
- Cholesterol 132 mg

Tasty Chicken Bites

Preparation Time: 10 minutes
Cooking Time: 10 minutes
Serve: 2

Ingredients:

- 1 lb chicken breasts, skinless, boneless and cut into cubes
- 2 tbsp fresh lemon juice
- 1 tbsp fresh oregano, chopped
- 2 tbsp olive oil
- 1/8 tsp cayenne pepper

Directions:

1. Place chicken in a bowl. Add reaming ingredients over chicken and mix well. Place chicken in the refrigerator for 1 hour.
2. Preheat the griddle to medium heat.
3. Spray griddle top with cooking spray.
4. Thread marinated chicken cubes onto the skewers.
5. Place skewers onto the hot griddle top and cook until chicken is completely done.
6. Serve and enjoy.

Nutritional Value (Amount per Serving):

- Calories 560
- Fat 31 g
- Carbohydrates 2 g
- Sugar 0.4 g
- Protein 66 g
- Cholesterol 202 mg

Zucchini Turkey Patties

Preparation Time: 10 minutes
Cooking Time: 10 minutes
Serve: 5

Ingredients:

- 1 lb ground turkey
- 1/4 cup breadcrumbs
- 6 oz zucchini, grated and squeezed out all liquid
- 1 tbsp onion, grated
- 1 garlic clove, grated
- Pepper
- Salt

Directions:

1. Add ground turkey and remaining ingredients into the bowl and mix until well combined.
2. Preheat the griddle to medium heat.
3. Spray griddle top with cooking spray.
4. Make patties from mixture and place onto the hot griddle top and cook until patties are golden brown from both sides.
5. Serve and enjoy.

Nutritional Value (Amount per Serving):

- Calories 190
- Fat 10 g
- Carbohydrates 1.8 g
- Sugar 0.7 g
- Protein 25 g
- Cholesterol 93 mg

Flavorful Chicken Kababs

Preparation Time: 10 minutes
Cooking Time: 15 minutes
Serve: 3

Ingredients:

- 2 chicken breasts, cut into cubes
- 1 onion, cut into quarters
- 1 bell pepper, cut into squares
- For marinade:
- 1 tsp nutmeg
- 1 tsp Italian seasoning
- 2 tsp sweet paprika
- 1/2 cup olive oil
- 1 lemon juice
- 2 garlic cloves, chopped
- 1/4 tsp cardamom
- 1/4 tsp paprika
- 1 tsp salt

Directions:

1. In a small bowl, mix together all marinade ingredients.
2. Add chicken, onions, and peppers in a large bowl.
3. Pour marinade over chicken and vegetables and coat well, cover, and place in the refrigerator for 1 hour.
4. Thread marinated chicken and vegetables onto the skewers.
5. Preheat the griddle to medium-low heat.
6. Spray griddle top with cooking spray.
7. Place skewers onto the hot griddle top and cook for 15 minutes or until chicken is cooked through. Turn skewers often.
8. Serve and enjoy.

Nutritional Value (Amount per Serving):

- Calories 515
- Fat 42 g
- Carbohydrates 8.2 g

- Sugar 4 g
- Protein 29 g
- Cholesterol 88 mg

Healthy Chicken Fajitas

Preparation Time: 10 minutes
Cooking Time: 15 minutes
Serve: 4

Ingredients:

- 2 chicken breasts, cut into chunks
- 2 carrots, sliced
- 2 zucchini, sliced
- 2 bell peppers, sliced
- 1 sweet potato, clean and cut into fries shape
- 1 tbsp olive oil
- 1/2 tsp dried oregano
- 1 tsp ground cumin
- 1 tbsp dried chives
- 2 tbsp paprika
- 1/4 tsp pepper
- 1 1/2 tsp salt

Directions:

1. Add all ingredients into the large mixing bowl and toss well.
2. Preheat the griddle to medium-low heat.
3. Spray griddle top with cooking spray.
4. Transfer chicken mixture onto the hot griddle top and cook until vegetables are tender and chicken is cooked.
5. Serve and enjoy.

Nutritional Value (Amount per Serving):

- Calories 255
- Fat 9.9 g
- Carbohydrates 19.1 g
- Sugar 8.4 g
- Protein 24.4 g
- Cholesterol 65 mg

Lemon Herb Chicken

Preparation Time: 10 minutes
Cooking Time: 12 minutes
Serve: 4

Ingredients:

- 4 chicken breasts, skinless and boneless
- 1/4 tsp garlic powder
- 1/2 tsp cumin
- 1/2 tsp dried oregano
- 1/2 tsp dried basil
- 1 tbsp olive oil
- 1 tbsp fresh lemon juice
- 1/2 tsp granulated sugar
- Pepper
- Salt

Directions:

1. In a small bowl, mix basil, oregano, cumin, garlic powder, and sugar.
2. Brush chicken breasts with oil from both sides and season with dry seasoning mix.
3. Preheat the griddle to high heat.
4. Spray griddle top with cooking spray.
5. Place chicken on hot griddle top and cook for 5-6 minutes.
6. Turn chicken to other side and cook for 5-6 minutes more.
7. Transfer chicken to the serving plate and drizzle with lemon juice.
8. Serve and enjoy.

Nutritional Value (Amount per Serving):

- Calories 310
- Fat 14 g
- Carbohydrates 1 g
- Sugar 0.6 g
- Protein 42 g
- Cholesterol 130 mg

Smoked Paprika Chicken

Preparation Time: 10 minutes

Cooking Time: 14 minutes

Serve: 3

Ingredients:

- 3 chicken breasts
- 2 tbsp olive oil
- 1/2 tsp cumin
- 2 tsp smoked paprika
- 1 tbsp fresh parsley, chopped
- 1 tbsp fresh lime juice
- 1/2 tsp salt

Directions:

1. In a bowl, combine together paprika, oil, cumin, and salt.
2. Add chicken to the bowl and mix well and set aside for 15 minutes.
3. Preheat the griddle to medium-low heat.
4. Spray griddle top with cooking spray.
5. Place chicken breasts on a hot griddle top and cook for 5-7 minutes then chicken and cook for 5-7 minutes.
6. Transfer chicken on serving plate and drizzle with lime juice.
7. Garnish with parsley and serve.

Nutritional Value (Amount per Serving):

- Calories 365
- Fat 20 g
- Carbohydrates 1 g
- Sugar 0.2 g
- Protein 42 g
- Cholesterol 130 mg

Tasty Chicken Fritters

Preparation Time: 10 minutes
Cooking Time: 10 minutes
Serve: 4

Ingredients:

- 1 lb ground chicken
- 1 tsp onion powder
- 1 tsp garlic powder
- 1/2 cup parmesan cheese, shredded
- 1 tbsp dill, chopped
- 1/2 cup breadcrumbs
- Pepper
- Salt

Directions:

1. Preheat the griddle to medium-low heat.
2. Spray griddle top with cooking spray.
3. Add all ingredients into the mixing bowl and mix until well combined.
4. Make patties from chicken mixture and place onto the hot griddle top and cook until golden brown from both sides.
5. Serve and enjoy.

Nutritional Value (Amount per Serving):

- Calories 310
- Fat 11 g
- Carbohydrates 12 g
- Sugar 1.3 g
- Protein 38 g
- Cholesterol 109 mg

Chapter 4: Beef, Pork & Lamb

Steak Kababs

Preparation Time: 10 minutes
Cooking Time: 15 minutes
Serve: 4

Ingredients:

- 1 lb beef sirloin, cut into 1-inch pieces
- 1 green bell pepper, cut into 1-inch pieces
- 1 cup mushrooms
- 1 tbsp fresh parsley, chopped
- 1 tsp garlic, minced
- 2 tsp olive oil
- 1 onion, cut into 1-inch pieces
- 3 tbsp butter
- Pepper
- Salt

Directions:

1. Preheat the griddle to medium-low heat.
2. Thread the beef, bell pepper, mushrooms, and onion onto the skewers.
3. Brush meat and vegetables with olive oil and season with pepper and salt.
4. Place skewers onto the hot griddle top and cook for 4-5 minutes per side.
5. Melt butter in a pan over medium-low heat.
6. Add garlic and sauté for a minute.
7. Remove pan from heat and stir in parsley, pepper, and salt.
8. Brush butter mixture all over kababs.
9. Serve and enjoy.

Nutritional Value (Amount per Serving):

- Calories 302
- Fat 20 g
- Carbohydrates 5 g
- Sugar 0 g
- Protein 25 g
- Cholesterol 0 mg

Flavors Lamb Chops

Preparation Time: 10 minutes
Cooking Time: 8 minutes
Serve: 6

Ingredients:

- 6 lamb chops
- 2 tbsp fresh mint, chopped
- 1/2 tsp Pepper
- 2 tbsp olive oil
- 1/2 tsp kosher salt

Directions:

1. Preheat the griddle to high heat.
2. Brush lamb chops with oil and season with pepper and salt.
3. Place lamb chops onto the hot griddle top and cook for 5 minutes.
4. Flip lamb chops and cook for 3 minutes.
5. Garnish with mint.
6. Serve and enjoy.

Nutritional Value (Amount per Serving):

- Calories 300
- Fat 19 g
- Carbohydrates 5 g
- Sugar 0 g
- Protein 25 g
- Cholesterol 0 mg

Easy Pork Chops

Preparation Time: 10 minutes

Cooking Time: 12 minutes

Serve: 4

Ingredients:

- 8 oz pork chops, boneless
- 1 tsp smoked paprika
- 1 tsp olive oil
- 1 tsp onion powder
- Pepper
- Salt

Directions:

1. Brush pork chops with oil.
2. Mix together remaining ingredients and rub over pork chops.
3. Preheat the griddle to high heat.
4. Place pork chops onto the hot griddle top and cook pork chops from both sides until completely done.
5. Serve and enjoy.

Nutritional Value (Amount per Serving):

- Calories 195
- Fat 15 g
- Carbohydrates 0.8 g
- Sugar 0.3 g
- Protein 13 g
- Cholesterol 49 mg

Tasty Beef Tips

Preparation Time: 10 minutes

Cooking Time: 12 minutes

Serve: 4

Ingredients:

- 1 lb rib-eye steak, cut into 1-inch cubes
- 1 tsp garlic powder
- 2 tbsp coconut aminos
- 2 tsp rosemary, crushed
- 1 tsp paprika
- 2 tsp onion powder
- Pepper
- Salt

Directions:

1. Add meat and remaining ingredients into the bowl and mix well cover and let it marinate for 10 minutes.
2. Preheat the griddle to medium-low heat.
3. Add the meat onto the hot griddle top and stir fry until cooked.
4. Serve and enjoy.

Nutritional Value (Amount per Serving):

- Calories 356
- Fat 24 g
- Carbohydrates 3.7 g
- Sugar 0.7 g
- Protein 29 g
- Cholesterol 95 mg

Beef Dill Patties

Preparation Time: 10 minutes

Cooking Time: 12 minutes

Serve: 4

Ingredients:

- 1 lb ground beef
- 1/8 tsp dried dill
- 1/2 tsp paprika
- 1/2 tsp dried dill
- 1/2 tsp onion powder
- 1/2 tsp garlic powder
- 2 tsp dried parsley
- Pepper
- Salt

Directions:

1. Add all ingredients into the large bowl and mix until well combined.
2. Preheat the griddle to medium-low heat.
3. Spray griddle top with cooking spray.
4. Make four even shape patties from meat mixture and place onto the hot griddle top and cook until golden brown from both sides.
5. Serve and enjoy.

Nutritional Value (Amount per Serving):

- Calories 215
- Fat 7.1 g
- Carbohydrates 0.7 g
- Sugar 0.2 g
- Protein 35 g
- Cholesterol 101 mg

Delicious Beef Kebabs

Preparation Time: 10 minutes

Cooking Time: 10 minutes

Serve: 4

Ingredients:

- 1 lb beef chuck ribs, cut into 1-inch pieces
- 1/2 onion, cut into 1-inch pieces
- 1 bell pepper, cut into 1-inch pieces
- 2 tbsp soy sauce
- 1/3 cup sour cream

Directions:

1. Add meat, soy sauce, and sour cream into the bowl and mix well.
2. Cover and place in the refrigerator overnight.
3. Thread marinated meat, onion, and bell peppers pieces onto the skewers.
4. Preheat the griddle to high heat.
5. Spray griddle top with cooking spray.
6. Place skewers onto the hot griddle top and cook until vegetables are tender and meat is completely cooked.
7. Serve and enjoy.

Nutritional Value (Amount per Serving):

- Calories 370
- Fat 30.2 g
- Carbohydrates 5 g
- Sugar 2.3 g
- Protein 20.6 g
- Cholesterol 84 mg

Steak & Mushrooms

Preparation Time: 10 minutes

Cooking Time: 15 minutes

Serve: 4

Ingredients:

- 1 lb steaks, cut into 1-inch cubes
- 8 oz mushrooms, halved
- 1/2 tsp garlic powder
- 1 tsp Worcestershire sauce
- 2 tbsp olive oil
- Pepper
- Salt

Directions:

1. Add steak cubes and remaining ingredients into the bowl and toss well.
2. Preheat the griddle to high heat.
3. Transfer meat mixture onto the hot griddle top and stir fry until meat is completely cooked.
4. Serve and enjoy.

Nutritional Value (Amount per Serving):

- Calories 300
- Fat 12 g
- Carbohydrates 2.4 g
- Sugar 1.3 g
- Protein 42.8 g
- Cholesterol 102 mg

Tasty Beef Fajitas

Preparation Time: 10 minutes

Cooking Time: 10 minutes

Serve: 4

Ingredients:

- 1 lb beef flank steak, sliced
- 1 red bell pepper, sliced
- 1 tsp garlic powder
- 1 tsp paprika
- 1 green bell peppers, sliced
- 1 1/2 tsp cumin
- 1/2 tbsp chili powder
- 3 tbsp olive oil
- Pepper
- Salt

Directions:

1. In a mixing bowl, toss sliced steak with remaining ingredients.
2. Preheat the griddle to high heat.
3. Transfer meat mixture onto the hot griddle top and cook until vegetables are tender and meat is cooked.
4. Serve and enjoy.

Nutritional Value (Amount per Serving):

- Calories 330
- Fat 18 g
- Carbohydrates 6.2 g
- Sugar 3 g
- Protein 35.5 g
- Cholesterol 101 mg

Healthy Beef & Broccoli

Preparation Time: 10 minutes
Cooking Time: 15 minutes
Serve: 2

Ingredients:

- 1/2 lb beef stew meat, cut into pieces
- 1/2 cup broccoli florets
- 1 onion, sliced
- 1 tbsp vinegar
- 1 garlic clove, minced
- 1 tbsp olive oil
- Pepper
- Salt

Directions:

1. Preheat the griddle to high heat.
2. Add meat and remaining ingredients into the large bowl and toss well and spread onto the hot griddle top.
3. Cook until broccoli is tender and meat is cooked.
4. Serve and enjoy.

Nutritional Value (Amount per Serving):

- Calories 305
- Fat 14 g
- Carbohydrates 7.3 g
- Sugar 2.8 g
- Protein 35.8 g
- Cholesterol 101 mg

Cheesy Beef Patties

Preparation Time: 10 minutes
Cooking Time: 12 minutes
Serve: 6

Ingredients:

- 2 lbs ground beef
- 1 tsp garlic powder
- 1 cup mozzarella cheese, grated
- 1 tsp onion powder
- Pepper
- Salt

Directions:

1. Add all ingredients into the large bowl and mix until well combined.
2. Preheat the griddle to high heat.
3. Spray griddle top with cooking spray.
4. Make patties from meat mixture and place onto the hot griddle top and cook until golden brown from both sides.
5. Serve and enjoy.

Nutritional Value (Amount per Serving):

- Calories 295
- Fat 10 g
- Carbohydrates 0.8 g
- Sugar 0.3 g
- Protein 47.3 g
- Cholesterol 138 mg

Easy Lemon Pepper Pork Chops

Preparation Time: 10 minutes
Cooking Time: 12 minutes
Serve: 4

Ingredients:

- 4 pork chops, boneless
- 1 tsp lemon pepper seasoning
- Salt

Directions:

1. Preheat the griddle to high heat.
2. Spray griddle top with cooking spray.
3. Season pork chops with lemon pepper seasoning, and salt and place onto the hot griddle top and cook for 5-7 minutes per side.
4. Serve and enjoy.

Nutritional Value (Amount per Serving):

- Calories 257
- Fat 20 g
- Carbohydrates 0.3 g
- Sugar 0 g
- Protein 18 g
- Cholesterol 69 mg

Ranch Pork Chops

Preparation Time: 10 minutes
Cooking Time: 15 minutes
Serve: 6

Ingredients:

- 6 pork chops, boneless
- 2 tbsp ranch seasoning, homemade
- 1/4 cup olive oil
- 1 tsp dried parsley
- Pepper
- Salt

Directions:

1. Preheat the griddle to high heat.
2. Spray griddle top with cooking spray.
3. Season pork chops with pepper and salt and place onto the hot griddle top.
4. Mix together olive oil, parsley, and ranch seasoning.
5. Spoon oil mixtures over pork chops and cook pork chops for 5-7 minutes per side.
6. Serve and enjoy.

Nutritional Value (Amount per Serving):

- Calories 328
- Fat 28.3 g
- Carbohydrates 0 g
- Sugar 0 g
- Protein 18 g
- Cholesterol 69 mg

Pork Chops with Potatoes

Preparation Time: 10 minutes

Cooking Time: 15 minutes

Serve: 4

Ingredients:

- 4 pork chops, boneless
- 1 oz ranch seasoning, homemade
- 2 1/2 lbs potatoes, cut into bite-size pieces
- 1/4 tsp pepper
- 1/4 tsp ground oregano
- 1 tsp dried parsley
- 3 tbsp olive oil

Directions:

1. Preheat the griddle to high heat.
2. Spray griddle top with cooking spray.
3. In a small bowl, mix together ranch seasoning mix, oregano, parsley, oil, and pepper.
4. Add potatoes and 1 1/2 tbsp seasoning mixture to the bowl and toss well.
5. Place potatoes onto the hot griddle top.
6. Season pork chops with remaining seasoning and place onto the griddle top along with potatoes.
7. Cook potatoes and pork chops until potatoes are tender and pork chops are completely cooked.
8. Serve and enjoy.

Nutritional Value (Amount per Serving):

- Calories 542
- Fat 30.7 g
- Carbohydrates 44.7 g
- Sugar 3.3 g
- Protein 22.8 g
- Cholesterol 69 mg

Rosemary Dijon Pork Chops

Preparation Time: 10 minutes
Cooking Time: 10 minutes
Serve: 4

Ingredients:

- 4 pork chops, boneless
- 2 tbsp fresh rosemary, chopped
- 1/4 cup Dijon mustard
- 1/4 cup coconut aminos
- 2 tbsp olive oil
- 1/2 tsp salt

Directions:

1. In a bowl, mix together rosemary, coconut aminos, olive oil, Dijon mustard, and salt.
2. Add pork chops to the bowl and coat well.
3. Cover and place in the refrigerator for 1 hour.
4. Preheat the griddle to high heat.
5. Spray griddle top with cooking spray.
6. Place marinated pork chops onto the hot griddle top and cook for 5 minutes on each side.
7. Serve and enjoy.

Nutritional Value (Amount per Serving):

- Calories 332
- Fat 27.8 g
- Carbohydrates 1.9 g
- Sugar 0.1 g
- Protein 18.7 g
- Cholesterol 69 mg

Greek Lamb Patties

Preparation Time: 10 minutes

Cooking Time: 8 minutes

Serve: 4

Ingredients:

- 1 lb ground lamb
- 5 basil leaves, minced
- 10 mint leaves, minced
- 1/4 cup fresh parsley, chopped
- 1 tsp dried oregano
- 1 cup feta cheese, crumbled
- 1 tbsp garlic, minced
- 1 jalapeno pepper, minced
- 1/4 tsp pepper
- 1/2 tsp kosher salt

Directions:

1. Add all ingredients into the mixing bowl and mix until well combined.
2. Preheat the griddle to high heat.
3. Spray griddle top with cooking spray.
4. Make four equal shape patties from meat mixture and place onto the hot griddle top and cook for 4 minutes on each side.
5. Serve and enjoy.

Nutritional Value (Amount per Serving):

- Calories 317
- Fat 16.4 g
- Carbohydrates 3 g
- Sugar 1.7 g
- Protein 37.5 g
- Cholesterol 135 mg

Easy Pork Kabab

Preparation Time: 10 minutes
Cooking Time: 8 minutes
Serve: 6

Ingredients:

- 2 lbs pork tenderloin, cut into 1-inch cubes
- 3 tbsp fresh parsley, chopped
- 1 tbsp garlic, chopped
- 1 onion, chopped
- 1/2 cup olive oil
- 1/2 cup vinegar
- Pepper
- Salt

Directions:

1. In a large zip-lock bag, mix vinegar, parsley, garlic, onion, and oil.
2. Add meat to bag and marinate in the refrigerator for overnight.
3. Thread marinated meat onto skewers. Season with pepper and salt.
4. Preheat the griddle to high heat.
5. Spray griddle top with cooking spray.
6. Place meat skewers onto the hot griddle top and cook for 3-4 minutes on each side.
7. Serve and enjoy.

Nutritional Value (Amount per Serving):

- Calories 375
- Fat 22 g
- Carbohydrates 2.5 g
- Sugar 1 g
- Protein 40 g
- Cholesterol 110 mg

Herb Beef Skewers

Preparation Time: 10 minutes
Cooking Time: 8 minutes
Serve: 4

Ingredients:

- 2 lbs beef sirloin, cut into cubes
- 2 tsp fresh thyme, minced
- 1 tbsp fresh parsley, minced
- 1 tbsp lemon zest
- 4 garlic cloves, minced
- 2 tbsp fresh lemon juice
- 1/4 cup olive oil
- 2 tsp dried oregano
- 2 tsp fresh rosemary, minced
- Pepper
- Salt

Directions:

1. Add all ingredients except meat in a mixing bowl and stir everything well.
2. Add meat to the bowl and coat well with marinade.
3. Place in refrigerator for overnight.
4. Preheat the griddle to high heat.
5. Spray griddle top with cooking spray.
6. Slide marinated meat onto the skewers.
7. Place skewers onto the hot griddle top and cook for 6-8 minutes. Turn after every 2 minutes.
8. Serve and enjoy.

Nutritional Value (Amount per Serving):

- Calories 543
- Fat 27 g
- Carbohydrates 2.7 g
- Sugar 0.3 g
- Protein 69.3 g
- Cholesterol 203 mg

Creole Pork Chops

Preparation Time: 10 minutes
Cooking Time: 10 minutes
Serve: 2

Ingredients:

- 2 pork chops
- 2 tsp Creole seasoning
- 2 tbsp fresh parsley, chopped
- 1/4 tsp pepper
- Salt

Directions:

1. Season pork chops with Creole seasoning, pepper, and salt.
2. Preheat the griddle to high heat.
3. Spray griddle top with cooking spray.
4. Place seasoned pork chops on hot griddle top and cook for 5 minutes.
5. Turn pork chops and cook for 5 minutes more.
6. Transfer pork chops on serving plate and garnish with parsley.
7. Serve and enjoy.

Nutritional Value (Amount per Serving):

- Calories 258
- Fat 19 g
- Carbohydrates 0.4 g
- Sugar 0 g
- Protein 18 g
- Cholesterol 69 mg

Lemon Oregano Lamb Chops

Preparation Time: 10 minutes
Cooking Time: 8 minutes
Serve: 4

Ingredients:

- 8 lamb chops
- 3 tbsp lemon juice
- 4 tbsp olive oil
- 3 garlic cloves, minced
- 2 tsp dried oregano
- 1/2 tsp pepper
- 1 tsp salt

Directions:

1. Add garlic, oregano, lemon juice, oil, pepper, and salt in a large bowl and mix well.
2. Add lamb chops in a bowl and coat well with marinade and set aside for 30 minutes.
3. Preheat the griddle to high heat.
4. Spray griddle top with cooking spray.
5. Place marinated lamb chops on hot griddle top and cook for 3-4 minutes on each side.
6. Serve and enjoy.

Nutritional Value (Amount per Serving):

- Calories 769
- Fat 65 g
- Carbohydrates 1.8 g
- Sugar 0.3 g
- Protein 38.4 g
- Cholesterol 160 mg

Beef Stir Fry

Preparation Time: 10 minutes
Cooking Time: 10 minutes
Serve: 4

Ingredients:

- 1 lb steak, sliced
- 4 tbsp coconut oil
- 1/2 lb broccoli, cut into florets
- 1 tsp fish sauce
- 1 tsp sesame oil
- For marinade:
- 4 tbsp coconut aminos
- 2 garlic cloves, chopped
- 1 tsp ginger, grated

Directions:

1. Add sliced meat to a zip-lock bag with garlic, ginger, and coconut aminos and let marinate for 1 hour.
2. Blanch broccoli in boiling water for 2 minutes. Drain well.
3. Drain marinated meat.
4. Preheat the griddle to high heat.
5. Spray griddle top with cooking spray.
6. Add marinated meat onto the hot griddle top and cook for 1-3 minutes or until browned.
7. Add broccoli and stir fry for 3 minutes.
8. Add fish sauce and sesame oil and stir well.
9. Serve and enjoy.

Nutritional Value (Amount per Serving):

- Calories 375
- Fat 20 g

- Saturated fat 14 g
- Carbohydrates 4 g
- Sugar 1.1 g
- Protein 42.8 g
- Cholesterol 102 mg

Chapter 5: Fish & Seafood

Salmon Zucchini Patties

Preparation Time: 10 minutes
Cooking Time: 10 minutes
Serve: 6

Ingredients:

- 2 eggs
- 1 1/2 lbs salmon, cooked
- 2 cups zucchini, shredded
- 2 tbsp onion, minced
- 1/4 cup fresh cilantro, chopped
- 1/4 cup olive oil
- 3/4 cup almond flour
- 3 tbsp fresh lime juice
- 2 tbsp jalapeno, minced
- 2 tsp salt

Directions:

1. Add salmon, lime juice, cilantro, zucchini, jalapenos, onion, eggs, and salt into the food processor and process until the mixture is combined.
2. Add almond flour to a shallow dish.
3. Preheat the griddle to high heat. Add oil to griddle.
4. Take 1/4 cup salmon mixture and form patties, coat patties with almond flour then place onto the hot griddle top and cook for 5 minutes per side.
5. Serve and enjoy.

Nutritional Value (Amount per Serving):

- Calories 330
- Fat 24 g
- Carbohydrates 5 g
- Sugar 1.5 g
- Protein 27.4 g
- Cholesterol 105 mg

Lemon Garlic Shrimp

Preparation Time: 10 minutes
Cooking Time: 15 minutes
Serve: 4

Ingredients:

- 1 1/2 lbs shrimp, peeled and deveined
- 1 tbsp garlic, minced
- 1/4 cup butter
- 1/4 cup fresh parsley, chopped
- 1/4 cup fresh lemon juice
- Pepper
- Salt

Directions:

1. Preheat the griddle to high heat.
2. Melt butter on the griddle top.
3. Add garlic and sauté for 30 seconds.
4. Add shrimp and season with pepper and salt and cook for 4-5 minutes or until it turns to pink.
5. Add lemon juice and parsley and stir well and cook for 2 minutes.
6. Serve and enjoy.

Nutritional Value (Amount per Serving):

- Calories 312
- Fat 14.6 g
- Carbohydrates 3.9 g
- Sugar 0.4 g
- Protein 39.2 g
- Cholesterol 389 mg

Flavorful Mexican Shrimp

Preparation Time: 10 minutes
Cooking Time: 12 minutes
Serve: 4

Ingredients:

- 1 lb shrimp, cleaned
- 3 tbsp fresh parsley, chopped
- 1 tbsp garlic, minced
- 1/4 onion, sliced
- 1/4 tsp paprika
- 1/4 tsp ground cumin
- 2 fresh lime juice
- 2 tbsp olive oil
- 1/4 cup butter
- Pepper
- Salt

Directions:

1. Season shrimp with paprika, cumin, pepper, and salt.
2. Preheat the griddle to high heat.
3. Add oil and butter to the griddle top.
4. Add onion and garlic and sauté for 5 minutes.
5. Add shrimp and cook for 5-8 minutes or until cooked.
6. Add parsley and lime juice.
7. Stir well and serve.

Nutritional Value (Amount per Serving):

- Calories 311
- Fat 20.5 g
- Carbohydrates 5 g
- Sugar 0.7 g
- Protein 26.4 g
- Cholesterol 269 mg

Pesto Shrimp

Preparation Time: 10 minutes

Cooking Time: 5 minutes

Serve: 4

Ingredients:

- 1 lb shrimp, remove shells and tails
- 1/2 cup basil pesto
- Pepper
- Salt

Directions:

1. Add shrimp, pesto, pepper, and salt into the large bowl and toss well. Set aside for 15 minutes.
2. Heat grill over medium-high heat.
3. Thread marinated shrimp onto the skewers and place onto the hot griddle top and cook for 1-2 minutes on each side.
4. Serve and enjoy.

Nutritional Value (Amount per Serving):

- Calories 270
- Fat 15 g
- Carbohydrates 3.7 g
- Sugar 2 g
- Protein 28.8 g
- Cholesterol 246 mg

Healthy Salmon Patties

Preparation Time: 10 minutes
Cooking Time: 10 minutes
Serve: 2

Ingredients:

- 6 oz can salmon, drained, remove bones, and pat dry
- 2 tbsp mayonnaise
- 1/2 cup almond flour
- 1/4 tsp thyme
- 1 egg, lightly beaten
- 2 tbsp olive oil
- Pepper
- Salt

Directions:

1. Add salmon, thyme, egg, mayonnaise, almond flour, pepper, and salt into the mixing bowl and mix until well combined.
2. Preheat the griddle to high heat.
3. Add oil to the griddle top.
4. Make small patties from salmon mixture and place onto the hot griddle top and cook for 5-6 minutes.
5. Turn patties and cook for 3-4 minutes more.
6. Serve and enjoy.

Nutritional Value (Amount per Serving):

- Calories 530
- Fat 41 g
- Carbohydrates 9.8 g
- Sugar 1.1 g
- Protein 30.6 g
- Cholesterol 146 mg

Blackened Salmon

Preparation Time: 10 minutes

Cooking Time: 10 minutes

Serve: 5

Ingredients:

- 1 1/4 lbs salmon fillets
- 2 tbsp blackened seasoning
- 2 tbsp butter

Directions:

1. Season salmon fillets with blackened seasoning.
2. Preheat the griddle to high heat.
3. Melt butter on the griddle top.
4. Place salmon fillets onto the hot griddle top and cook for 4-5 minutes.
5. Turn salmon and cook for 4-5 minutes more.
6. Serve and enjoy.

Nutritional Value (Amount per Serving):

- Calories 190
- Fat 11 g
- Carbohydrates 0 g
- Sugar 0 g
- Protein 21.1 g
- Cholesterol 62 mg

Blackened Tilapia

Preparation Time: 10 minutes
Cooking Time: 6 minutes
Serve: 4

Ingredients:

- 4 tilapia fillets
- 2 tbsp butter
- 1 tbsp olive oil
- For seasoning:
- 1 1/2 tsp paprika
- 1 lemon, sliced
- 1/2 tsp ground cumin
- 1 tsp oregano
- 1/2 tsp garlic powder
- Pepper
- Salt

Directions:

1. In a small bowl, mix together all seasoning ingredients and rub over fish fillets.
2. Preheat the griddle to high heat.
3. Add butter and oil on the hot griddle top.
4. Place fish fillets onto the griddle top and cook for 3 minutes.
5. Turn fish fillets and cook for 3 minutes more or until cooked through.
6. Serve and enjoy.

Nutritional Value (Amount per Serving):

- Calories 181
- Fat 10.5 g
- Carbohydrates 1.2 g
- Sugar 0.2 g
- Protein 21.4 g
- Cholesterol 70 mg

Italian Shrimp

Preparation Time: 10 minutes
Cooking Time: 5 minutes
Serve: 4

Ingredients:

- 1 lb shrimp, deveined
- 1 tsp Italian seasoning
- 1 tsp paprika
- 1 1/2 tsp garlic, minced
- 1 stick butter
- 1 fresh lemon juice
- 1/4 tsp pepper
- 1/2 tsp salt

Directions:

1. Preheat the griddle to high heat.
2. Melt butter on the hot griddle top.
3. Add garlic and cook for 30 seconds.
4. Toss shrimp with paprika, Italian seasoning, pepper, and salt.
5. Add shrimp into the pan and cook for 2-3 minutes per side.
6. Drizzle lemon juice over shrimp.
7. Stir and serve.

Nutritional Value (Amount per Serving):

- Calories 346
- Fat 25 g
- Carbohydrates 2.6 g
- Sugar 0.2 g
- Protein 26.2 g
- Cholesterol 300 mg

Shrimp Veggie Stir Fry

Preparation Time: 10 minutes
Cooking Time: 10 minutes
Serve: 2

Ingredients:

- 1/2 lb shrimp, peeled and deveined
- 1 tbsp garlic, minced
- 1/3 cup olives
- 1 cup mushrooms, sliced
- 2 tbsp olive oil
- 1 cup tomatoes, diced
- 1 small onion, chopped
- Pepper
- Salt

Directions:

1. Preheat the griddle to high heat. Add oil.
2. Add onion, mushrooms, and garlic and sauté until onion soften.
3. Add shrimp and tomatoes and stir until shrimp is cooked through.
4. Add olives and stir well.
5. Remove pan from heat and set aside for 5 minutes. Season with pepper and salt.
6. Serve and enjoy.

Nutritional Value (Amount per Serving):

- Calories 325
- Fat 18.7 g
- Carbohydrates 12.5 g
- Sugar 4.5 g
- Protein 28.6 g
- Cholesterol 239 mg

Lemon Garlic Scallops

Preparation Time: 10 minutes
Cooking Time: 5 minutes
Serve: 2

Ingredients:

- 1 lb frozen bay scallops, thawed, rinsed & pat dry
- 1 tsp garlic, minced
- 2 tbsp olive oil
- 1 tsp parsley, chopped
- 1 tsp lemon juice
- Pepper
- Salt

Directions:

1. Preheat the griddle to high heat.
2. Add oil to the griddle top.
3. Add garlic and sauté for 30 seconds.
4. Add scallops, lemon juice, pepper, and salt, and sauté until scallops turn opaque.
5. Garnish with parsley and serve.

Nutritional Value (Amount per Serving):

- Calories 123
- Fat 14 g
- Carbohydrates 0.6 g
- Sugar 0.1 g
- Protein 0.1 g
- Cholesterol 0 mg

Tasty Shrimp Skewers

Preparation Time: 10 minutes
Cooking Time: 7 minutes
Serve: 6

Ingredients:

- 1 1/2 lbs shrimp, peeled and deveined
- 1 tbsp dried oregano
- 2 tsp garlic paste
- 2 lemon juice
- 1/4 cup olive oil
- 1 tsp paprika
- Pepper
- Salt

Directions:

1. Add all ingredients into the mixing bowl and mix well and place in the refrigerator for 1 hour.
2. Remove marinated shrimp from refrigerator and thread onto the skewers.
3. Preheat the griddle to high heat.
4. Place skewers onto the griddle top and cook for 5-7 minutes.
5. Serve and enjoy.

Nutritional Value (Amount per Serving):

- Calories 212
- Fat 10.5 g
- Carbohydrates 2.7 g
- Sugar 0.1 g
- Protein 26 g
- Cholesterol 239 mg

Balsamic Salmon

Preparation Time: 10 minutes
Cooking Time: 10 minutes
Serve: 6

Ingredients:

- 6 salmon fillets
- 5 tbsp balsamic vinaigrette
- 2 tbsp olive oil
- 1 1/2 tsp garlic powder
- Pepper
- Salt

Directions:

1. In a mixing bowl, add salmon, garlic powder, balsamic vinaigrette, pepper, and salt and mix well. Set aside.
2. Preheat the griddle to high heat.
3. Add oil to the hot griddle top.
4. Place salmon onto the griddle top and cook for 3-5 minutes on each side or until cooked through.
5. Serve and enjoy.

Nutritional Value (Amount per Serving):

- Calories 328
- Fat 20.7 g
- Carbohydrates 1.4 g
- Sugar 1 g
- Protein 34.7 g
- Cholesterol 78 mg

Paprika Garlic Shrimp

Preparation Time: 10 minutes

Cooking Time: 5 minutes

Serve: 4

Ingredients:

- 1 lb shrimp, peeled and cleaned
- 5 garlic cloves, chopped
- 2 tbsp olive oil
- 1 tbsp fresh parsley, chopped
- 1 tsp paprika
- 2 tbsp butter
- 1/2 tsp sea salt

Directions:

1. Add shrimp, 1 tbsp oil, garlic, and salt in a large bowl and toss well and place in the refrigerator for 1 hour.
2. Preheat the griddle to high heat.
3. Add remaining oil and butter on the hot griddle top.
4. Once butter is melted then add marinated shrimp and paprika and stir constantly for 2-3 minutes or until shrimp is cooked.
5. Garnish with parsley and serve.

Nutritional Value (Amount per Serving):

- Calories 253
- Fat 15 g
- Carbohydrates 3.3 g
- Sugar 0.1 g
- Protein 26.2 g
- Cholesterol 254 mg

Spicy Lemon Butter Shrimp

Preparation Time: 10 minutes
Cooking Time: 10 minutes
Serve: 4

Ingredients:

- 1 1/2 lbs shrimp, peeled and deveined
- 3 garlic cloves, minced
- 1 small onion, minced
- 1/2 cup butter
- 1 1/2 tbsp fresh parsley, chopped
- 1 tbsp fresh lemon juice
- 1/4 tsp red pepper flakes
- Pepper
- Salt

Directions:

1. Preheat the griddle to high heat.
2. Melt butter on the griddle top.
3. Add garlic, onion, red chili flakes, pepper, and salt and stir for 2 minutes.
4. Season shrimp with pepper and salt and thread onto skewers.
5. Brush shrimp skewers with butter mixture.
6. Place shrimp skewers on griddle top and cook until shrimp turns to pink, about 3-4 minutes.
7. Transfer shrimp to the serving plate.
8. Drizzle lemon juice over shrimp and garnish with parsley.
9. Serve and enjoy.

Nutritional Value (Amount per Serving):

- Calories 419
- Fat 25 g
- Carbohydrates 5.2 g
- Sugar 0.9 g
- Protein 39.4 g
- Cholesterol 419 mg

Greek Salmon

Preparation Time: 10 minutes
Cooking Time: 6 minutes
Serve: 2

Ingredients:

- 12 oz salmon, cut into two pieces
- 1 tsp Greek seasoning
- 1 tbsp olive oil
- 1/2 tsp lemon zest
- 1 garlic clove, minced
- Pepper
- Salt

Directions:

1. In a large bowl, mix olive oil, lemon zest, garlic, pepper, salt, and greek seasoning.
2. Add salmon in a bowl and coat well with marinade and set aside for 15 minutes.
3. Preheat the griddle to high heat.
4. Place marinated salmon on hot griddle top and cook for 2-3 minutes.
5. Turn salmon to the other side and cook for 2-3 minutes more.
6. Serve and enjoy.

Nutritional Value (Amount per Serving):

- Calories 290
- Fat 17.6 g
- Carbohydrates 1.4 g
- Sugar 0.1 g
- Protein 33.2 g
- Cholesterol 75 mg

Garlic Butter Tilapia

Preparation Time: 10 minutes
Cooking Time: 8 minutes
Serve: 6

Ingredients:

- 2 lbs tilapia fillets
- 1 tsp garlic powder
- 1/2 fresh lemon juice
- 1 tbsp butter, melted
- Pepper
- Salt

Directions:

1. In a small bowl, combine together lemon juice, garlic powder, and butter and microwave for 10 seconds.
2. Brush both the side of the fish fillet with lemon mixture. Season fillet with pepper and salt.
3. Preheat the griddle to high heat.
4. Spray griddle top with cooking spray.
5. Place fillets on hot griddle top and cook for 4 minutes on each side.
6. Serve and enjoy.

Nutritional Value (Amount per Serving):

- Calories 143
- Fat 3 g
- Carbohydrates 0.4 g
- Sugar 0.1 g
- Protein 28.2 g
- Cholesterol 79 mg

Caper Basil Halibut

Preparation Time: 10 minutes

Cooking Time: 8 minutes

Serve: 4

Ingredients:

- 24 oz halibut fillets
- 2 garlic cloves, crushed
- 2 tbsp olive oil
- 2 tsp capers, drained
- 3 tbsp fresh basil, sliced
- 2 1/2 tbsp fresh lemon juice

Directions:

1. In a small bowl, whisk together garlic, olive oil, and lemon juice. Stir in 2 tbsp basil.
2. Season garlic mixture with pepper and salt.
3. Season fish fillets with pepper and salt and brush with garlic mixture.
4. Preheat the griddle to high heat.
5. Place fish fillets on hot griddle and cook for 4 minutes on each side.
6. Transfer fish fillets on serving plate and top with remaining garlic mixture and basil.
7. Serve and enjoy.

Nutritional Value (Amount per Serving):

- Calories 250
- Fat 10.5 g
- Carbohydrates 0.8 g
- Sugar 0.2 g
- Protein 39.1 g
- Cholesterol 59 mg

Greek Salmon Fillets

Preparation Time: 10 minutes

Cooking Time: 6 minutes

Serve: 2

Ingredients:

- 2 salmon fillets
- 1 tbsp fresh basil, minced
- 1 tbsp butter, melted
- 1 tbsp fresh lemon juice
- 1/8 tsp salt

Directions:

1. Preheat the griddle to high heat.
2. In a small bowl, mix together lemon juice, basil, butter, and salt.
3. Brush salmon fillets with lemon mixture and place them on the hot griddle top.
4. Cook salmon for 2-3 minutes. Flip salmon and cook for 2-3 minutes more.
5. Serve and enjoy.

Nutritional Value (Amount per Serving):

- Calories 290
- Fat 16.8 g
- Carbohydrates 0.3 g
- Sugar 0.2 g
- Protein 34.7 g
- Cholesterol 46 mg

Salmon Skewers

Preparation Time: 10 minutes
Cooking Time: 10 minutes
Serve: 4

Ingredients:

- 1 lb salmon fillets, cut into 1-inch cubes
- 2 tbsp soy sauce
- 1 tbsp toasted sesame seeds
- 1 lime zest
- 2 tsp olive oil
- 1 1/2 tbsp maple syrup
- 1 tsp ginger, crushed
- 1 lime juice

Directions:

1. In a bowl, mix together olive oil, soy sauce, lime zest, lime juice, maple syrup, and ginger.
2. Add salmon and stir to coat. Set aside for 10 minutes.
3. Preheat the griddle to high heat.
4. Slide marinated salmon pieces onto the skewers and cook on a hot griddle top for 8-10 minutes or until cooked through.
5. Sprinkle salmon skewers with sesame seeds and serve.

Nutritional Value (Amount per Serving):

- Calories 209
- Fat 10 g
- Carbohydrates 6.5 g
- Sugar 4.6 g
- Protein 22.9 g
- Cholesterol 50 mg

Parmesan Shrimp

Preparation Time: 10 minutes
Cooking Time: 6 minutes
Serve: 4

Ingredients:

- 1 lb shrimp, peeled and deveined
- 2 tbsp parmesan cheese, grated
- 1 tbsp fresh lemon juice
- 1 tbsp pine nuts, toasted
- 1 garlic clove
- 1/2 cup basil
- 1 tbsp olive oil
- Pepper
- Salt

Directions:

1. Add basil, lemon juice, cheese, pine nuts, garlic, pepper, and salt in a blender and blend until smooth.
2. Add shrimp and basil paste in a bowl and mix well.
3. Place shrimp bowl in the fridge for 20 minutes.
4. Preheat the griddle to high heat.
5. Spray griddle top with cooking spray.
6. Thread marinated shrimp onto skewers and place skewers on the hot griddle top.
7. Cook shrimp for 3 minutes on each side or until cooked.
8. Serve and enjoy.

Nutritional Value (Amount per Serving):

- Calories 225
- Fat 11.2 g
- Carbohydrates 2.2 g
- Sugar 0.2 g
- Protein 27.2 g
- Cholesterol 241 mg

Chapter 6: Vegetable & Side Dishes

Stir Fry Mushrooms

Preparation Time: 10 minutes
Cooking Time: 10 minutes
Serve: 2

Ingredients:

- 10 oz mushrooms, sliced
- 1/4 cup olive oil
- 1 tbsp garlic, minced
- 1/4 tsp dried thyme
- Pepper
- Salt

Directions:

1. Preheat the griddle to high heat.
2. Add 2 tablespoons of oil to the hot griddle top.
3. Add mushrooms, garlic, thyme, pepper, and salt and sauté mushrooms until tender.
4. Drizzle remaining oil and serve.

Nutritional Value (Amount per Serving):

- Calories 253
- Fat 25.6 g
- Carbohydrates 6.2 g
- Sugar 2.5 g
- Protein 4.7 g
- Cholesterol 0 mg

Stir Fry Vegetables

Preparation Time: 10 minutes
Cooking Time: 20 minutes
Serve: 4

Ingredients:

- 2 medium potatoes, cut into small pieces
- 3 medium carrots, peeled and cut into small pieces
- 1/4 cup olive oil
- 1 small rutabaga, peeled and cut into small pieces
- 2 medium parsnips, peeled and cut into small pieces
- Pepper
- Salt

Directions:

1. Preheat the griddle to high heat.
2. In a large bowl, toss vegetables with olive oil.
3. Transfer vegetables onto the hot griddle top and stir fry until vegetables are tender.
4. Serve and enjoy.

Nutritional Value (Amount per Serving):

- Calories 218
- Fat 12.8 g
- Carbohydrates 25.2 g
- Sugar 6.2 g
- Protein 2.8 g
- Cholesterol 0 mg

Easy Fried Rice

Preparation Time: 10 minutes
Cooking Time: 10 minutes
Serve: 2

Ingredients:

- 4 cups rice, cooked
- 2 large eggs
- 2 tbsp green onion, sliced
- 2 tbsp olive oil
- 1 tsp salt

Directions:

1. In a bowl, whisk eggs and set aside.
2. Preheat the griddle to high heat.
3. Spray griddle top with cooking spray.
4. Add cooked rice on hot griddle top and fry until rice separate from each other.
5. Push rice to one side of the griddle top. Add oil to the griddle and pour beaten egg.
6. Add salt and mix egg quickly with rice and cook until rice grains are covered by egg.
7. Add green onion and stir fry for 2 minutes.
8. Serve and enjoy.

Nutritional Value (Amount per Serving):

- Calories 557
- Fat 19.8 g
- Carbohydrates 79.6 g
- Sugar 0.7 g
- Protein 14 g
- Cholesterol 186 mg

Healthy Zucchini Noodles

Preparation Time: 10 minutes

Cooking Time: 10 minutes

Serve: 4

Ingredients:

- 4 small zucchini, spiralized
- 1 tbsp soy sauce
- 2 onions, spiralized
- 2 tbsp olive oil
- 1 tbsp sesame seeds
- 2 tbsp teriyaki sauce

Directions:

1. Preheat the griddle to high heat.
2. Add oil to the hot griddle top.
3. Add onion and sauté for 4-5 minutes.
4. Add zucchini noodles and cook for 2 minutes.
5. Add sesame seeds, teriyaki sauce, and soy sauce and cook for 4-5 minutes.
6. Serve and enjoy.

Nutritional Value (Amount per Serving):

- Calories 124
- Fat 8.4 g
- Carbohydrates 11.3 g
- Sugar 5.7 g
- Protein 3.2 g
- Cholesterol 0 mg

Easy Seared Green Beans

Preparation Time: 10 minutes
Cooking Time: 10 minutes
Serve: 6

Ingredients:

- 1 1/2 lbs green beans, trimmed
- 1 1/2 tbsp rice vinegar
- 3 tbsp soy sauce
- 1 1/2 tbsp sesame oil
- 2 tbsp sesame seeds, toasted
- 1 1/2 tbsp brown sugar
- 1/4 tsp black pepper

Directions:

1. Cook green beans in boiling water for 3 minutes and drain well.
2. Transfer green beans to chilled ice water and drain again. Pat dry green beans.
3. Preheat the griddle to high heat.
4. Add oil to the hot griddle top.
5. Add green beans and stir fry for 2 minutes.
6. Add soy sauce, brown sugar, vinegar, and pepper and stir fry for 2 minutes more.
7. Add sesame seeds and toss well to coat.
8. Serve and enjoy.

Nutritional Value (Amount per Serving):

- Calories 100
- Fat 5 g
- Carbohydrates 11.7 g
- Sugar 3.9 g
- Protein 3.1 g
- Cholesterol 0 mg

Stir Fry Bok Choy

Preparation Time: 10 minutes

Cooking Time: 5 minutes

Serve: 4

Ingredients:

- 2 heads bok choy, trimmed and cut crosswise
- 1 tsp sesame oil
- 2 tsp soy sauce
- 2 tbsp water
- 1 tbsp butter
- 1 tbsp peanut oil
- 1 tbsp oyster sauce
- 1/2 tsp salt

Directions:

1. In a small bowl, mix together soy sauce, oyster sauce, sesame oil, and water and set aside.
2. Preheat the griddle to high heat.
3. Add oil to the hot griddle top.
4. Add bok choy and salt and stir fry for 2 minutes.
5. Add butter and soy sauce mixture and stir fry for 1-2 minutes.
6. Serve and enjoy.

Nutritional Value (Amount per Serving):

- Calories 122
- Fat 8.2 g
- Carbohydrates 9.5 g
- Sugar 5 g
- Protein 6.5 g
- Cholesterol 8 mg

Sautéed Vegetables

Preparation Time: 10 minutes

Cooking Time: 5 minutes

Serve: 4

Ingredients:

- 2 medium zucchini, cut into matchsticks
- 2 tbsp coconut oil
- 2 tsp garlic, minced
- 1 tbsp honey
- 3 tbsp soy sauce
- 1 tsp sesame seeds
- 2 cups carrots, cut into matchsticks
- 2 cups snow peas

Directions:

1. In a small bowl, mix together soy sauce, garlic, and honey and set aside.
2. Preheat the griddle to high heat.
3. Add oil to the hot griddle top.
4. Add carrots, snow peas, and zucchini, and sauté for 1-2 minutes.
5. Add soy sauce mixture and stir fry for 1 minute.
6. Garnish with sesame seeds and serve.

Nutritional Value (Amount per Serving):

- Calories 160
- Fat 7.5 g
- Carbohydrates 20.2 g
- Sugar 12.1 g
- Protein 5.3 g
- Cholesterol 0 mg

Stir Fry Cabbage

Preparation Time: 10 minutes

Cooking Time: 5 minutes

Serve: 4

Ingredients:

- 1 cabbage head, tear cabbage leaves, washed and drained
- 2 green onion, sliced
- 1 tbsp ginger, minced
- 2 garlic cloves, minced
- 1 tbsp soy sauce
- 1/2 tbsp vinegar
- 4 dried chilies
- 2 tbsp olive oil
- 1/2 tsp salt

Directions:

1. Preheat the griddle to high heat.
2. Add oil to the hot griddle top.
3. Add ginger, garlic, and green onion and sauté for 2-3 minutes.
4. Add dried chilies and sauté for 30 seconds.
5. Add cabbage, vinegar, soy sauce, and salt and stir fry for 1-2 minutes over high heat until cabbage wilted.
6. Serve and enjoy.

Nutritional Value (Amount per Serving):

- Calories 115
- Fat 7.3 g
- Carbohydrates 12.7 g
- Sugar 6 g
- Protein 2.9 g
- Cholesterol 0 mg

Pineapple Fried Rice

Preparation Time: 10 minutes
Cooking Time: 10 minutes
Serve: 4

Ingredients:

- 3 cups cooked brown rice
- 1/2 cup frozen corn
- 2 carrots, peeled and grated
- 1 onion, diced
- 2 garlic cloves, minced
- 2 tbsp olive oil
- 1/2 tsp ginger powder
- 1 tbsp sesame oil
- 3 tbsp soy sauce
- 1/4 cup green onion, sliced
- 1/2 cup ham, diced
- 2 cups pineapple, diced
- 1/2 cup frozen peas

Directions:

1. In a small bowl, whisk soy sauce, ginger powder, and sesame oil and set aside.
2. Preheat the griddle to high heat.
3. Add oil to the hot griddle top.
4. Add onion and garlic and sauté for 3-4 minutes.
5. Add corn, carrots, and peas and stir constantly for 3-4 minutes.
6. Stir in cooked rice, green onions, ham, pineapple, and soy sauce mixture and stir continuously for 2-3 minutes.
7. Serve and enjoy.

Nutritional Value (Amount per Serving):

- Calories 375
- Fat 13.3 g
- Carbohydrates 57.6 g
- Sugar 12.7 g
- Protein 9.4 g
- Cholesterol 10 mg

Italian Zucchini Slices

Preparation Time: 10 minutes
Cooking Time: 5 minutes
Serve: 4

Ingredients:

- 2 zucchini, cut into 1/2-inch thick slices
- 1 tsp Italian seasoning
- 2 garlic cloves, minced
- 1/4 cup butter, melted
- 1 1/2 tbsp fresh parsley, chopped
- 1 tbsp fresh lemon juice
- Pepper
- Salt

Directions:

1. In a small bowl, mix melted butter, lemon juice, Italian seasoning, garlic, pepper, and salt.
2. Brush zucchini slices with melted butter mixture.
3. Preheat the griddle to high heat.
4. Place zucchini slices on the griddle top and cook for 2 minutes per side.
5. Transfer zucchini slices on serving plate and garnish with parsley.
6. Serve and enjoy.

Nutritional Value (Amount per Serving):

- Calories 125
- Fat 12 g
- Carbohydrates 4.1 g
- Sugar 1.9 g
- Protein 1.5 g
- Cholesterol 31 mg

Chapter 7: Snacks

Cripsy Eggplant Bites

Preparation Time: 10 minutes
Cooking Time: 10 minutes
Serve: 4

Ingredients:

- 1 eggplant, cut into 1-inch pieces
- 2 tbsp olive oil
- 1/2 tsp Italian seasoning
- 1 tsp paprika
- 1/2 tsp red pepper
- 1 tsp garlic powder

Directions:

1. Add all ingredients into the large bowl and toss well.
2. Preheat the griddle to high heat.
3. Spray griddle top with cooking spray.
4. Transfer eggplant mixture onto the hot griddle top and cook until eggplant pieces are crispy.
5. Serve and enjoy.

Nutritional Value (Amount per Serving):

- Calories 100
- Fat 7.5 g
- Carbohydrates 8.7 g
- Sugar 4.5 g
- Protein 1.5 g
- Cholesterol 0 mg

Tasty Cauliflower Skewers

Preparation Time: 10 minutes
Cooking Time: 14 minutes
Serve: 6

Ingredients:

- 1 large cauliflower head, cut into florets
- 1 onion, cut into wedges
- 1 yellow bell pepper, cut into squares
- 1 fresh lemon juice
- 3 tsp curry powder
- 1/4 cup olive oil
- 1/2 tsp garlic powder
- 1/2 tsp ground ginger
- 1/2 tsp salt

Directions:

1. In a large bowl, whisk together oil, lemon juice, garlic, ginger, curry powder, and salt.
2. Add cauliflower florets and toss until well coated.
3. Preheat the griddle to high heat.
4. Spray griddle top with cooking spray.
5. Thread cauliflower florets, onion, and bell pepper onto the skewers.
6. Place skewers onto the hot griddle top and cook for 6-7 minutes on each side.
7. Serve and enjoy.

Nutritional Value (Amount per Serving):

- Calories 125
- Fat 8 g
- Carbohydrates 11 g
- Sugar 5 g
- Protein 3.4 g
- Cholesterol 0 mg

Flavors Cauliflower Bites

Preparation Time: 10 minutes

Cooking Time: 10 minutes

Serve: 4

Ingredients:

- 1 lb cauliflower florets
- 1 tsp ground coriander
- 1/2 tsp dried rosemary
- 1 1/2 tsp garlic powder
- 1 tbsp olive oil
- 1 tsp sesame seeds
- Pepper
- Salt

Directions:

1. Preheat the griddle to high heat.
2. Spray griddle top with cooking spray.
3. Add cauliflower florets and remaining ingredients into the bowl and toss well and spread on the hot griddle top.
4. Cook cauliflower florets until tender.
5. Serve and enjoy.

Nutritional Value (Amount per Serving):

- Calories 65
- Fat 4 g
- Carbohydrates 7.1 g
- Sugar 3 g
- Protein 2.6 g
- Cholesterol 0 mg

Tasty Herb Mushrooms

Preparation Time: 10 minutes

Cooking Time: 10 minutes

Serve: 4

Ingredients:

- 1 lb mushroom caps
- 1 tbsp basil, minced
- 1 garlic clove, minced
- 1/2 tbsp vinegar
- 1/2 tsp ground coriander
- 1 tsp rosemary, chopped
- Pepper
- Salt

Directions:

1. Preheat the griddle to high heat.
2. Spray griddle top with cooking spray.
3. Add all ingredients into the bowl and toss well.
4. Add mushroom mixture onto the hot griddle top and cook until mushroom is tender.
5. Serve and enjoy.

Nutritional Value (Amount per Serving):

- Calories 25
- Fat 0.4 g
- Carbohydrates 4 g
- Sugar 2 g
- Protein 3.6 g
- Cholesterol 0 mg

Cauliflower Zucchini Fritters

Preparation Time: 10 minutes
Cooking Time: 8 minutes
Serve: 4

Ingredients:

- 2 medium zucchini, grated and squeezed
- 1 tbsp olive oil
- 1/4 cup coconut flour
- 3 cups cauliflower rice
- 1/2 tsp sea salt

Directions:

1. Add all ingredients except oil into the bowl and mix until well combined.
2. Preheat the griddle to high heat.
3. Add oil to the hot griddle top.
4. Make small patties from the mixture and place onto the griddle top and cook for 3-4 minutes on each side.
5. Serve and enjoy.

Nutritional Value (Amount per Serving):

- Calories 90
- Fat 5 g
- Carbohydrates 8.8 g
- Sugar 5 g
- Protein 4.3 g
- Cholesterol 0 mg

Parmesan Zucchini Patties

Preparation Time: 10 minutes

Cooking Time: 30 minutes

Serve: 6

Ingredients:

- 1 cup zucchini, shredded and squeeze out all liquid
- 1/2 tbsp Dijon mustard
- 1 egg, lightly beaten
- 1/4 tsp red pepper flakes
- 1/4 cup parmesan cheese, grated
- 1/2 tbsp mayonnaise
- 1/2 cup breadcrumbs
- 2 tbsp onion, minced
- Pepper
- Salt

Directions:

1. Add all ingredients into the bowl and mix until well combined.
2. Preheat the griddle to high heat.
3. Spray griddle top with cooking spray.
4. Make small patties from the zucchini mixture and place on hot griddle top and cook until golden brown from both sides.
5. Serve and enjoy.

Nutritional Value (Amount per Serving):

- Calories 156
- Fat 7.7 g
- Carbohydrates 7.9 g
- Sugar 1.2 g
- Protein 10.5 g
- Cholesterol 48 mg

Stir Fry Potatoes & Carrots

Preparation Time: 10 minutes

Cooking Time: 15 minutes

Serve: 2

Ingredients:

- 1/2 lb potatoes, cut into 1-inch cubes
- 1/2 onion, diced
- 1/2 tsp Italian seasoning
- 1/4 tsp garlic powder
- 1/2 lb carrots, peeled & cut into chunks
- 1 tbsp olive oil
- Pepper
- Salt

Directions:

1. In a large bowl, toss carrots, potatoes, garlic powder, Italian seasoning, oil, onion, pepper, and salt.
2. Preheat the griddle to high heat.
3. Spray griddle top with cooking spray.
4. Transfer carrot potato mixture on hot griddle top and cook until tender.
5. Serve and enjoy.

Nutritional Value (Amount per Serving):

- Calories 201
- Fat 7.5 g
- Carbohydrates 32 g
- Sugar 8.2 g
- Protein 3.2 g
- Cholesterol 1 mg

Ranch Potatoes

Preparation Time: 10 minutes

Cooking Time: 12 minutes

Serve: 2

Ingredients:

- 1/2 lb baby potatoes, wash and cut in half
- 1/4 tsp garlic powder
- 1/2 tbsp olive oil
- 1/4 tsp dill
- 1/4 tsp chives
- 1/4 tsp parsley
- 1/4 tsp paprika
- 1/4 tsp onion powder
- Salt

Directions:

1. Preheat the griddle to high heat.
2. Spray griddle top with cooking spray.
3. Add all ingredients into the mixing bowl and toss well.
4. Spread potatoes on hot griddle top and cook until tender.
5. Serve and enjoy.

Nutritional Value (Amount per Serving):

- Calories 100
- Fat 3.7 g
- Carbohydrates 14.8 g
- Sugar 0.2 g
- Protein 3.1 g
- Cholesterol 0 mg

Yummy Turkey Burger

Preparation Time: 10 minutes
Cooking Time: 14 minutes
Serve: 6

Ingredients:

- 1 lb ground turkey
- 1 egg, lightly beaten
- 1 cup Monterey jack cheese, grated
- 1 cup carrot, grated
- 1 cup cauliflower, grated
- 2 garlic cloves, minced
- 1/2 cup onion, minced
- 3/4 cup breadcrumbs
- Pepper
- Salt

Directions:

1. Preheat the griddle to high heat.
2. Spray griddle top with cooking spray.
3. Add all ingredients into the mixing bowl and mix until well combined.
4. Make small patties from mixture and place on hot griddle top and cook until golden brown from both sides.
5. Serve and enjoy.

Nutritional Value (Amount per Serving):

- Calories 299
- Fat 15.5 g
- Carbohydrates 13.8 g
- Sugar 2.7 g
- Protein 2.7 g
- Cholesterol 121 mg

Broccoli Fritters

Preparation Time: 10 minutes
Cooking Time: 12 minutes
Serve: 4

Ingredients:

- 2 eggs, lightly beaten
- 3 cups broccoli florets, steam & chopped
- 2 garlic cloves, minced
- 2 cups mozzarella cheese, shredded
- 1/4 cup breadcrumbs
- Pepper
- Salt

Directions:

1. Preheat the griddle to high heat.
2. Spray griddle top with cooking spray.
3. Add all ingredients into the large bowl and mix until well combined.
4. Make patties from broccoli mixture and place on hot griddle top and cook until golden brown from both sides.
5. Serve and enjoy.

Nutritional Value (Amount per Serving):

- Calories 124
- Fat 5.3 g
- Carbohydrates 10.6 g
- Sugar 1.8 g
- Protein 9.7 g
- Cholesterol 89 mg

Chapter 8: Game Recipes

Flavorful Cornish Game Hen

Preparation Time: 10 minutes

Cooking Time: 60 minutes

Serve: 2

Ingredients:

- 1 cornish game hen
- 1/2 tbsp olive oil
- 1/4 tbsp poultry seasoning

Directions:

1. Brush hen with oil and rub with poultry seasoning.
2. Preheat the griddle to high heat.
3. Spray griddle top with cooking spray.
4. Place hen on hot griddle top and cook from all the sides until brown.
5. Cover hen with lid or pan and cook for 60 minutes or until the internal temperature of hen reaches 180 F.
6. Slice and serve.

Nutritional Value (Amount per Serving):

- Calories 366
- Fat 26.9 g
- Carbohydrates 0.3 g
- Sugar 0 g
- Protein 28 g
- Cholesterol 168 mg

Flavorful Marinated Cornish Hen

Preparation Time: 10 minutes

Cooking Time: 60 minutes

Serve: 2

Ingredients:

- 1 cornish hen
- 1 cup cold water
- 16 oz apple juice
- 1/8 cup brown sugar
- 1 cinnamon stick
- 1 cup hot water
- 1/4 cup kosher salt

Directions:

1. Add cinnamon, hot water, cold water, apple juice, brown sugar, and salt into the large pot and stir until sugar is dissolved.
2. Add hen in the brine and place in the refrigerator for 4 hours.
3. Preheat the griddle to high heat.
4. Spray griddle top with cooking spray.
5. Remove hens from brine and place on hot griddle top and cook for 60 minutes or until internal temperature reaches 160 F.
6. Slice and serve.

Nutritional Value (Amount per Serving):

- Calories 938
- Fat 9.5 g
- Carbohydrates 232 g
- Sugar 200 g
- Protein 10 g
- Cholesterol 51 mg

Montreal Seasoned Spatchcocked Hens

Preparation Time: 10 minutes
Cooking Time: 60 minutes
Serve: 2

Ingredients:

- 1 cornish hen
- 1 tbsp olive oil
- 1 tbsp Montreal chicken seasoning

Directions:

1. Cut the backbone of hens and flatten the breastplate.
2. Brush hen with oil and rub with Montreal chicken seasoning.
3. Wrap hens in plastic wrap and place in the refrigerator for 4 hours.
4. Preheat the griddle to high heat.
5. Spray griddle top with cooking spray.
6. Place marinated hen on hot griddle top and cook for 60 minutes or until internal temperature reaches 180 F.
7. Serve and enjoy.

Nutritional Value (Amount per Serving):

- Calories 228
- Fat 18 g
- Carbohydrates 0 g
- Sugar 0 g
- Protein 14 g
- Cholesterol 85 mg

Rosemary Hen

Preparation Time: 10 minutes
Cooking Time: 60 minutes
Serve: 2

Ingredients:

- 1 cornish game hen
- 1 tbsp butter, melted
- 1/2 tbsp rosemary, minced
- 1 tsp chicken rub

Directions:

1. Brush hens with melted butter.
2. Mix together rosemary and chicken rub.
3. Rub hen with rosemary and chicken rub mixture.
4. Preheat the griddle to high heat.
5. Spray griddle top with cooking spray.
6. Place hen on hot griddle top and cook for 60 minutes or until internal temperature reaches 165 F.
7. Serve and enjoy.

Nutritional Value (Amount per Serving):

- Calories 221
- Fat 17 g
- Carbohydrates 0.5 g
- Sugar 0 g
- Protein 14.5 g
- Cholesterol 100 mg

BBQ Hen

Preparation Time: 10 minutes
Cooking Time: 1 hour 30 minutes
Serve: 8

Ingredients:

- 1 cornish hen
- 2 tbsp BBQ rub

Directions:

1. Preheat the griddle to high heat.
2. Spray griddle top with cooking spray.
3. Coat hens with BBQ rub and place on hot griddle top and cook for 1 1/2 hours or until the internal temperature of hens reach 165 F.
4. Slice and serve.

Nutritional Value (Amount per Serving):

- Calories 168
- Fat 11 g
- Carbohydrates 0 g
- Sugar 0 g
- Protein 14 g
- Cholesterol 85 mg

Honey Garlic Cornish Hen

Preparation Time: 10 minutes

Cooking Time: 60 minutes

Serve: 2

Ingredients:

- 1 cornish hen
- 2 garlic cloves, minced
- 1/8 cup honey
- 1/4 cup soy sauce
- 3/4 cup warm water
- 1 tbsp cornstarch
- 1/4 cup brown sugar

Directions:

1. Mix together soy sauce, warm water, brown sugar, garlic, cornstarch, and honey.
2. Place Cornish hen in baking dish and season with pepper and salt.
3. Pour marinade over hen and place in the refrigerator for 10 hours.
4. Preheat the griddle to high heat.
5. Spray griddle top with cooking spray.
6. Place marinated hen on hot griddle top and cook for 60 minutes or until internal temperature reaches 165 F.
7. Serve and enjoy.

Nutritional Value (Amount per Serving):

- Calories 338
- Fat 11.8 g
- Carbohydrates 42.3 g
- Sugar 35.6 g
- Protein 16.6 g
- Cholesterol 85 mg

Sage Thyme Cornish Hen

Preparation Time: 10 minutes
Cooking Time: 60 minutes
Serve: 2

Ingredients:

- 1 cornish hen
- 1/2 tbsp paprika
- 1/4 tsp pepper
- 1/4 tsp sage
- 1/2 tsp thyme
- 1/2 tbsp onion powder

Directions:

1. In a small bowl, mix together paprika, onion powder, thyme, sage, and pepper.
2. Rub hen with paprika mixture.
3. Preheat the griddle to high heat.
4. Spray griddle top with cooking spray.
5. Place hen on hot griddle top and cook for 60 minutes or until internal temperature reaches 185 F.
6. Serve and enjoy.

Nutritional Value (Amount per Serving):

- Calories 180
- Fat 12 g
- Carbohydrates 2.7 g
- Sugar 0.8 g
- Protein 14.9 g
- Cholesterol 85 mg

Asian Cornish Hen

Preparation Time: 10 minutes

Cooking Time: 60 minutes

Serve: 2

Ingredients:

- 1 cornish hen
- 1 1/2 tsp Chinese five-spice powder
- 1 1/2 tsp rice wine
- 1/2 tsp pepper
- 2 cups of water
- 3 tbsp soy sauce
- 2 tbsp sugar
- Salt

Directions:

1. In a large bowl, mix together water, soy sauce, sugar, rice wine, five-spice, pepper, and salt.
2. Place Cornish hen in the bowl and place in the refrigerator for overnight.
3. Preheat the griddle to high heat.
4. Spray griddle top with cooking spray.
5. Remove Cornish hen from marinade and place on hot griddle top and cook for 60 minutes or until internal temperature reaches 185 F.
6. Slice and serve.

Nutritional Value (Amount per Serving):

- Calories 233
- Fat 11.8 g
- Carbohydrates 15.9 g
- Sugar 13.4 g
- Protein 15.9 g
- Cholesterol 85 mg

Orange Cornish Hen

Preparation Time: 10 minutes
Cooking Time: 60 minutes
Serve: 2

Ingredients:

- 1 cornish hen
- 1/4 onion, cut into chunks
- 1/4 orange cut into wedges
- 2 garlic cloves
- 4 fresh sage leaves
- 1 1/2 fresh rosemary sprigs
- For glaze:
- 2-star anise
- 1 tbsp honey
- 1 cup orange juice
- 1/4 fresh orange, sliced
- 1/2 orange zest
- 1.5 oz Grand Marnier
- 1/2 cinnamon stick

Directions:

1. Stuff hen with orange wedges, garlic, onions, and herbs. Season with pepper and salt.
2. Preheat the griddle to high heat.
3. Spray griddle top with cooking spray.
4. Place hen on hot griddle top and cook for 60 minutes or until the internal temperature of hens reaches 165 F.
5. Meanwhile, in a saucepan heat, all glaze ingredients until reduce by half over medium-high heat.
6. Brush hen with glaze.

7. Slice and serve.

Nutritional Value (Amount per Serving):

- Calories 351
- Fat 12.1 g
- Carbohydrates 29.2 g
- Sugar 40.9 g
- Protein 16 g
- Cholesterol 85 mg

Rosemary Butter Cornish Hens

Preparation Time: 10 minutes
Cooking Time: 60 minutes
Serve: 2

Ingredients:

- 1 cornish hen, rinse and pat dry with paper towels
- 1 tbsp butter, melted
- 1 rosemary sprigs
- 1 tsp poultry seasoning

Directions:

1. Stuff rosemary sprigs into the hen cavity.
2. Brush hen with melted butter and season with poultry seasoning.
3. Preheat the griddle to high heat.
4. Spray griddle top with cooking spray.
5. Place hen on hot griddle top and cook for 60 minutes or until the internal temperature of hens reaches 165 F.
6. Slice and serve.

Nutritional Value (Amount per Serving):

- Calories 127
- Fat 8 g
- Carbohydrates 0.5 g
- Sugar 0 g
- Protein 13 g
- Cholesterol 74 mg

Conclusion

The Blackstone griddle is founded and started to manufacture different types of the griddle in 2005. They manufactured flagship griddle and the product made by Blackstone are bestseller products available in the market. The quality of products is the design and manufactured in the USA. In this book, we have used Blackstone outdoor gas griddle to cook delicious griddle dishes.

The book contains 100 delicious and tasty recipes from different categories like breakfast, poultry, beef pork and lamb, fish and seafood, vegetables and side dishes, snacks, and game recipes. All the recipes are unique and written in an easily understandable form. The recipes are written with their number of servings, preparation, and cooking time information. Each recipe ends with its exact nutritional value information.

CPSIA information can be obtained
at www.ICGtesting.com
Printed in the USA
BVHW022008230623
666303BV00009B/170

9 781954 091177